10 DATING

SECRETS

THAT WORK

Finding a MAN WORTH Keeping

HOWARD
PUBLISHING CO.

VICTORYA MICHAELS ROGERS

OUR PURPOSE AT HOWARD PUBLISHING IS TO:

- *Increase faith* in the hearts of growing Christians
- *Inspire holiness* in the lives of believers
- *Instill hope* in the hearts of struggling people everywhere

BECAUSE HE'S COMING AGAIN!

Finding a Man Worth Keeping © 2005 by Victorya Michaels Rogers
All rights reserved. Printed in the United States of America
Published by Howard Publishing Co., Inc.
3117 North Seventh Street, West Monroe, Louisiana 71291-2227
www.howardpublishing.com
In association with the literary agency of Alive Communications, Inc.
7680 Goddard Street, Suite 200, Colorado Springs, Colorado 80920

06 07 08 09 10 11 12 13 14   10 9 8 7 6 5 4 3

Edited by Michele Buckingham
Interior design by John Mark Luke Designs
Cover design by Terry Dugan

Library of Congress Cataloging-in-Publication Data

Rogers, Victorya Michaels.
    Finding a man worth keeping : 10 dating secrets that work / Victorya Michaels Rogers.
        p. cm.
    Includes bibliographical references.
    ISBN 1-58229-449-6
        1. Dating (Social customs) 2. Man-woman relationships. I. Title.

HQ801.R634 2005
646.7'7'082—dc22

2005046268

For more information about Victorya Michaels Rogers, go to www.victoryamichaelsrogers .com and www.finderskeepersclub.com.

For

Christine and *Kirsten*

you are prizes worth winning.
May God quickly bring you
your men worth keeping!

ABOUT THE *Author*

VICTORYA MICHAELS ROGERS

Author and speaker Victorya Michaels Rogers spent more than a decade as a Hollywood agent, representing award-winning writers, producers, directors, actors, and technical crews. She also taught three years for the Entertainment Extension Program at UCLA. Victorya earned her bachelor's degree from California State University at Long Beach and her master's degree in theology from Fuller Theological Seminary. Currently Rogers is a motivational speaker and author and is the coauthor of *The Day I Met God* and *How to Talk about Jesus without Freaking Out*. Victorya speaks to audiences across America and lives in Oklahoma with her husband, Will, and children, Matthew and Katie. For more information about Victorya, go to www.victoryamichaelsrogers.com.

Contents

THANK YOU vii

INTRODUCTION: HOW THE SECRETS CAME TO BE 1

SECRET 1: FIND OUT WHAT YOU WANT. 13

SECRET 2: TURN YOUR LIFE INSIDE OUT 27

SECRET 3: TAKE AN HONEST LOOK IN THE MIRROR 49

SECRET 4: LET THE WORLD KNOW YOU'RE FREE. 75

SECRET 5: SEEK DIVINE INTERVENTION 95

SECRET 6: BE A GREAT DATE 113

SECRET 7: DON'T FREAK HIM OUT 133

SECRET 8: KNOW YOUR LIMITS 151

SECRET 9: FACE REALITY 163

SECRET 10: CALL IT LOVE OR CALL IT QUITS 185

EPILOGUE: TOMORROW IS ANOTHER DAY 203

BONUS SECTION: EXTRA SECRETS FOR SINGLE MOMS. . . . 207

NOTES. 215

Thank You

This book is the fulfillment of my dream to give back to searching single women the same vital hope and encouragement I received during my challenging single years. Just as I could never have thrived during those trying times had I embarked on that journey alone, I could never have written this book without the prayer and support of my amazing family and friends. So here's to all my cheerleaders.

During my single years: thanks to my mom, Sandra Sterud; my sister, Teri Rippeon; and to Peri Bayazit, Lori Beenam, Cathy Brown, Laura Cacciatore, Donna Cherry, Karen Covell, Christine Devine, Linnea Hance, Vickie Holland, Cheryl Jewell, Linda Lunney, Lynn Rosenthal, Abby Sheeline, Kellie Stade, Nancy Stafford, Jennifer Sterud, and Pam Wilson, to name just a few.

Thanks to all my friends who read my manuscript, gave honest feedback, and cheered me on during the writing phase: Kelly and Phil Free, Cheri Fuller, Stephanie Garza, Robin Marsh, Kirsten

McIntyre, Amy Mcree, Pam Whitley, and especially Karen Covell and Melanie Hemry, who encouraged me as I wrote each and every page. You all kept me going when I thought I couldn't do it!

Thanks also to all my girlfriends who graciously allowed me to share their lives with you; to Lee Hough for introducing me to Howard Publishing; to my talented, wise, and enthusiastic editor, Michele Buckingham; and to Philis and Denny Boultinghouse, John and Chrys Howard, Gary Myers, and the Howard Publishing family for believing in me and my vision.

All my love to Will, my very own "man worth keeping," for matching my husband wish list, choosing to marry me, and allowing me to share our life together with the world.

Last, but not least, to my Lord and Savior Jesus Christ: thank you for the amazing life you've given me, including a loving family, a wonderful husband, and two precious children. Above all else, thank you for choosing *and* keeping me!

HOW THE SECRETS
Came to Be

When I was a little girl, I dreamed of getting married, having kids, and living happily ever after. I wanted the fairy tale. At age five I was ready for a husband! As I grew up, I prayed earnestly for him to appear. Certainly God would honor my consistent requests and come through for me, right?

Wrong. *Decades* passed with no husband. In fact, I didn't have my first "official" boyfriend (one who would claim he was actually dating me) until I was *twenty-one*. And I was moments away from *thirty-five* when I finally walked down the aisle of holy matrimony to long-awaited wedded bliss.

Between those years I earned a bachelor's degree in journalism and a master's degree in theology; but what I deserved most was an honorary PhD in dating. I devoured dozens upon dozens of books on dating and the psychology of relationships. I got lots of trial-and-error, hands-on experience; made many naive and often painful mistakes; and spent many long hours in persevering prayer. I topped off my dating education by observing glamorous models, movie stars, and other women who were actively pursued by appealing men during my career as a Hollywood agent. I watched. I studied. And I learned.

The result? During my twenties and thirties, I dated more than one hundred men—ninety-seven of whom asked me out for a second date. I *know* the secrets for attracting a man. More importantly, I know the secrets for finding, dating, and keeping the *right* man!

Was it always fun during my active dating years? No. Did I always get a third, fourth, or fifth date? No. Did I cry often? Absolutely. But every step of the way, I learned and I grew. And now, after more than seven years of marriage, I can honestly say without hesitation that my husband, Will, is worth every tear I ever shed over a boy—and believe me, there were barrels full!

Through exhilarating highs and devastating lows, I finally triumphed in the soap opera of my personal single life by diligently practicing the secrets I am about to share with you in this book. You can triumph too. Believe me, I've been there. I know your struggle. I know your tears. I've walked in your shoes. That's why I want to talk with you openly, honestly, and practically in the pages that follow, not as some kind of clinical expert armed with theories and statistics, but rather as a friend—a girlfriend who truly wants you to have what I have: the man of my dreams.

SOMETIMES PEOPLE DON'T SAY THE RIGHT THING

I was having lunch one day with a handsome Christian D.J. who was in his early forties. I was thirty. It didn't take long to figure out why he was still single. Though he loved God dearly, he couldn't forgive himself for dodging the draft during the Vietnam War. I tried my best to be helpful by emphasizing God's grace, but he just didn't want to hear it.

"Don't you get it?" he finally snapped at me. "Just as a woman is not a woman if she hasn't had children by thirty, a man is not a man if he hasn't seen combat!"

All-righty, then. I get it now . . .

My lunch date was not the first person to say the wrong thing to me during my single years. Have you noticed that people rarely seem to say the right thing to single women? Do any of the following comments sound familiar?

"Why are *you* still single?"

"Better hurry up if you want children."

"You're too picky."

"Oh, you'll find someone. Just pray about it."

"Maybe you're too needy."

"You're trying too hard."

"Maybe God is trying to teach you something first."

"Stop looking, and God will bring you someone when he's ready."

I could go on and on. Sadly, well-meaning Christians are often the ones who say the most hurtful things. Their words sting, especially when you feel you've been doing everything possible to make yourself worthy of a spouse—from getting right with God to becoming a great catch. Yet your dream mate still eludes you.

Does any of this strike a chord? Then this is the book for you! The secrets I'm about to reveal will not only help you find your man worth keeping, they will also help you discover the exciting plans God has had for your life all along. You can actually begin being happy and single right now, even as you move forward toward your goal of wedded bliss.

MY STORY

As I mentioned earlier, when I was little girl, all I ever dreamed about was getting married, having babies, and living happily ever after. I would play house for hours, imagining what my life would be like when I grew up. I was raised in a Christian home with a mom and dad who held hands and kissed. I wanted to have that one day! But for a long time, it seemed that God had other plans.

Jesus was very real to me back then. In fact, he has been a very real part of my life for as long as I can remember. Still, I was very insecure as a young girl. I was absolutely terrified of rejection, confrontation, and conflict. In school I became a goody-two-shoes, straight-and-narrow type. I didn't know how to be popular. I wasn't pretty, so the boys didn't notice me—which, through my preteen and teenage years, kept my confidence level at the bottom of the sea. I specifically remember walking into the girls' bathroom in junior high as the pretty girls were primping and saying to myself, "Oh, if only I could be pretty like them, *then* the boys would like me." I had the pity-party thing down pat.

I spent my high-school years being a "buddy" to the guys and staying at home on date nights. Being a buddy was great, but I wanted a *date*. I was sick of being a friend. I wanted lips! Do you know what I mean? I wanted to be asked out to a movie or dinner or a football game on a Friday night—not spend my time dreaming about it. But dreaming was all I got. My date calendar was nil, zilch. We're talking a real joke. I can count the number of dates I had throughout junior high and high school on one hand.

In those years and on into my college years, I was so hungry for love that I searched for it everywhere, from the sappy pages of romance novels to the scandalous soap operas on TV. All the beautiful women on the soaps seemed to have beautiful men falling madly in love with them. In my own life, I felt invisible; but these beautiful women were anything but. Excitement followed them wherever they went. Sure, their relationships were filled with constant trauma, cheating, and deceit; but they were "in love." How wonderful!

Thankfully I got over my soap-opera delusions by my midtwenties, and I gave up my unhealthy addiction to daytime TV. Otherwise, who knows what soap-opera look-alike I would have ended up with? Most likely he would have been a gorgeous, needy, self-absorbed womanizer—basically, every real woman's nightmare.

I went to college mostly to look for my MRS degree. Instead of a husband, however, I left college four years later with a degree in journalism. Shortly thereafter I began my career in Hollywood. And finally, at twenty-one, I found my first real boyfriend. Wow! *I finally mattered!* I was no longer invisible. I had my own "Tom Cruise," and for the first time in my life, I didn't have to daydream about a fantasy relationship.

But the real world doesn't always work like the fantasy world. Lord knows I tried to make things work; but after two and a half years, I walked away from boyfriend number one and decided to focus on my career. *If I become a successful Hollywood agent, I figured, I'm sure to be around more eligible bachelors.*

By twenty-three, I was promoted to an executive position at a prestigious Beverly Hills talent agency. As my career took off, so did my search for beauty and physical perfection, *à la* Hollywood. I was convinced that if I learned how to be beautiful—if I learned the walk and the talk—men would fall all over me. Then my Friday nights would finally be filled with fabulous men in Mercedes-Benz cars and Armani suits.

And to my amazement, it worked! For the first time in my life, dating men became a busy, wonderful, exciting hobby for me. I was even pursued by a Grammy Award–winning rock star, an Academy Award–winning actor, and a top country singer. But in every case, I came up empty. My ego was stroked, but none of those men was my prince.

Of course, I was working in a field that is not known for Christian values or a large number of Christian men. Handsome, talented men were everywhere, but most of them didn't hold the values I sought in a husband. For that reason, whenever I did find a Christian man to date, I jumped in quickly—often too quickly— thinking, *This must be it!* Since we shared the same faith, I assumed we shared all the same values, desires, and goals. Big mistake. Those were my most devastating breakups, because I had expected so much.

"Christians aren't perfect, just forgiven." Man, did I learn the truth of that statement! Yet each time a Christian man broke my heart, I blamed God.

In desperation I began to "missionary date"—you know, go out with non-Christians and hope they find Jesus. Pretty dumb! I experienced heartbreak after heartbreak with men I should never have dated in the first place. The fact that my own choices brought the pain was little consolation. In fact, after each breakup, I managed to get mad at God rather than at myself. Hadn't I begged him to bring me a husband? I was simply trying to help him out since he was too busy to deliver.

Always in hindsight, though, I realized how blessed I was that God had said no to this one or that one. Have you ever looked back on an old relationship and wanted to sing, like Garth Brooks, "I thank God for unanswered prayers"?

By my thirties, many Prince Charmings had come and gone. Two engagements had slipped through my fingers. Still, I continued to press on in my quest for true love. *It's not over until you give up*, I told myself often—although by that point, I was pretty sure God wanted me to be single forever. After all, even though I yearned desperately for a husband, I *was* living a rich and fulfilling single life. I had a wonderful career and many friends. I traveled internationally. I had time to earn my master's degree. I managed to keep living— and I discovered that I was happy. Yes, I was alone, but I was living the abundant life Jesus promised in John 10:10: "The thief comes only to steal and kill and destroy; I have come that they may have life, and have it to the full."

What more could I ask?

Then it *happened.* In January of 1996, I attended the Golden Globe Awards at the Beverly Hilton Hotel. A handsome businessman from Oklahoma just happened to be staying there. He approached a girlfriend of mine and asked to see her program. She snapped at him, and he just laughed. My friend was so charmed that she immediately took him under her wing. She managed to sneak him into the ballroom and the after-show parties. She also happened to introduce him to me.

At the time I had no interest in a cute guy from Oklahoma. Not only was he geographically undesirable, but Brad Pitt, Tom Cruise, and Kevin Costner were in the next room. Would *you* care?

Yet God's plan would not be deterred. Ten months later, the man from Oklahoma came back to Los Angeles and invited me to lunch. It was love at second sight. Will and I were married exactly two years after our first meeting.

I have to tell you, waiting on God's best was the hardest—and best—choice I ever made in my life. But it wasn't a one-time decision. I had to make that choice again and again and again. Throughout the melodrama of my single years, no matter how hard I tried to force God's hand, his timing never seemed to be my timing. I had to learn to trust that his plan was the best plan for me.

AVOIDING THE EXTREMES

It wasn't easy, but I held firmly to two foundational truths during those years:

1. God is in control and has a personal plan for my life.

2. I'd rather be happy and alone than married and lonely.

I often said that second truth out loud to myself—especially when I was feeling particularly desperate for a husband. I've seen far too many lonely married people. I was determined not to be one of them.

Have you ever wondered why so many Christian women seem to end up either single and unhappy or married and lonely? Perhaps it is their approach to the whole dating process. After all, how we view and approach any subject greatly affects how we will experience it.

When it comes to the search for a husband, there are two flawed schools of thought among Christians today. The first is that you should simply wait on God, sit at home, and twiddle your thumbs. Your prince will miraculously appear on your doorstep, and you will live happily ever after—all with no effort on your part.

Come on, now! I'm not saying God couldn't give you a burning-bush experience in the wilderness of your husband search. But more than likely, if you think like that, you'll end up alone. Clearly we're to seek God's will daily in every area of our lives—including our choice of a mate. We're to believe and have faith he is working out his perfect plan. But do *nothing*? That's not even biblical!

Here are just three examples of faithful women in the Bible who showed their faith by their *action*:

- Ruth, a young widow with little hope of finding another husband, chose to be faithful and obedient to her mother-in-law, Naomi. Each day she stooped in backbreaking labor to glean food from a field to feed herself and her mother-in-law. Eventually Boaz, the field's owner, noticed her, and the two were married. Because she was faithful and active, Ruth not only found a wonderful husband, she became the great-grandmother of King David and an ancestor of Jesus Christ.

- Before Esther was chosen by King Xerxes to be queen, she was obedient to her cousin, Mordecai, and submitted herself to the king's selection process. Even though she was already beautiful, she agreed to undergo twelve months of additional beauty treatments. As a result, not only did she win the king's heart, she was in the right place at the right time to save the entire Jewish nation from an evil annihilation plot.

- Mary faithfully believed the angel of God when he told her she would give birth to the Messiah. But she didn't stop there; she actively obeyed the angel and married Joseph, even though she had to endure ridicule for carrying an "illegitimate" baby and then travel with great discomfort to Joseph's hometown of Bethlehem. As a result, she had a husband who was a good man from the line of King David. And in due time, she gave birth to Jesus, the Savior of the whole world.

Throughout the Bible, men and women alike showed their faith in God by obedience and action. These three single women certainly weren't thumb-twiddlers. They didn't sit at home doing nothing while they waited for God to drop a husband in their laps.

The second school of thought is equally flawed: that you should try to make something happen on your own and leave God out of the dating equation. After all, isn't he too busy with more important things, like saving the world? This thinking is easily proven disastrous by noting one fact: the current divorce rate *inside* the church is just as high as the divorce rate *outside* the church. How tragic! Apparently, simply being Christian doesn't make any of us smart enough to pick and stick with a mate.

YOU DO YOUR PART; GOD WILL DO HIS

So how involved should God be in the process of choosing your husband? Extremely! Include God in every aspect of your dating life. He cares. And while you're seeking God, keep moving forward and doing your part. As James 2:26 says, "The body is dead when there is no spirit in it. It is the same with faith. Faith is dead when nothing is done" (NLV). Make plans and take action, knowing that God is ready, willing, and able to intervene and direct your steps if you are willing to let him.[1] Believe he has a personal plan for your life. And if that plan includes marriage, it certainly includes *whom* you will marry!

The bottom line is that in the process of finding a man worth keeping, God has his part, and you have yours. That's why I've written this book: to help you focus on your part while persistently trusting God to do his.

I have to be honest with you. These ten secrets I'm about to share are tough to put into practice. (If they were easy, you'd already be married, right?) There's no twiddling of thumbs in these pages! Finding the right man to marry—a man you truly love and who loves you back; a man who shares your values, your faith, and your dreams; a man who recognizes how blessed he is to have found *you*—will take total commitment and dedication to yourself and to God. But the end result will be worth every ounce of effort you put into the process. I promise!

Girlfriend, no matter your past mistakes, no matter your current situation, there is hope for you! I believe that, and I want you to believe it too. I started writing this book more than ten years ago, when I was still single. At that point I truly didn't know if God was going to grace me with a wonderful husband—*ever*. But I clung to that hope, drew closer to God, found comfort in the Bible, and stuck to the dating secrets I had discovered. Sure, I fell on my knees during many tear-drenched sessions and cried on the shoulders of countless girlfriends. But I kept holding out for Mr. Wonderful, *not* Mr. Man-in-Front-of-Me-Right-Now. And boy, am I glad I did!

My prayer is that you will do the same. Don't give up, and don't settle! If you follow my ten secrets and invite God to direct your steps in the process, I can almost guarantee that you will find an incredible man worth keeping.

And what if you don't? After all, marriage is not definitively God's plan for everyone. Still, if you follow all ten of my secrets and, in spite of everything, remain single, you will nonetheless be so much better off! You will have embarked on a wonderful journey of self-discovery. You will have developed a deeper, more intimate relationship with God. And you will have learned how to live a happy, full, and fulfilling life—with or without a husband.

So before you turn another page, stop right now, memorize your two new mission statements, and determine to repeat them often:

1. God is in control and has a personal plan for my life.

2. I'd rather be happy and alone than married and lonely.

Bon voyage!

FIND OUT WHAT You Want

How Stacy's heart melted every time her boyfriend of six months showed up at her front door! He was gorgeous, fit, funny, charming, and he *loved* Stacy. Never mind that he had no idea what he was going to do with his life career-wise. Yes, he could be a little controlling and critical at times, but he was *so* sweet. And while it was true he was divorced with two young kids and in debt deeper than he could calculate, he thought Stacy was great and wanted to marry her—music to Stacy's ears!

Still, something was not quite right. Stacy couldn't put her finger on it, but something inside her felt hollow every time they were together. At least she had a man who wanted to marry her, right? Wasn't that enough?

Have you ever felt like Stacy? Just thrilled that someone finally noticed you or flattered you? Forget the fact that he's a mess inside and far from the ideal mate.

But wait. *Hello.* You can't forget! That's the whole purpose of this book—to help you wake up, face reality, and get on a path toward finding a man worth keeping for the rest of your life. Believe me, heartbreak now is better than the realization later that you married the wrong mate.

Too often the formula for dating and marriage goes like this: girl yearns for love; girl meets boy; girl experiences instant attraction as inexplicable fireworks go off inside her head; girl and boy become inseparable and addicted to one another—much like a person becomes dependent on Diet Coke, alcohol, or drugs to maintain a certain "feel-good" sensation. And since being together "feels right," girl ignores any negative signs that might warn her that something is wrong with this picture. After all, the boy says he loves her, so he must be "the one." Hence, girl blindly walks down the aisle—and ends up married and lonely, living for years with someone with whom she has nothing in common but fading passion.

You don't have to be that girl! But you risk being that girl if you don't know what you're looking for ahead of time. To recognize your man when he finally shows up, you must first take the time to discover what you really want in a mate. That's the first secret to finding a man worth keeping. Sound simple? You'd be amazed at how many women I meet who are clueless about what they really want in their man!

To get you started on secret 1, we're going to do two eye-opening exercises right up front to immediately remove any potential you may have for falling into the "clueless" category. The first exercise is a reality check that will help answer the question, What have you been getting thus far in your love life? Maybe you've done a great job attracting some of the worst men on the planet. Don't you think it's time to start attracting some good ones? The second exercise will help answer the question, what do you really want in a mate? You need to know what you *really* want in your husband *before* you walk down that aisle—in fact, before you go on your next date! By the time you finish the second exercise, I think you'll have a good idea of all you have to gain and what little you have to lose by following the ten dating secrets in this book.

The truth is, if you want to catch a man worth keeping, you have to first be absolutely committed to yourself and your own needs. Yes, that's right—sometimes it *is* all about you! The wisest man who ever lived once said, "There is a time for everything, and a season for every activity under heaven" (Ecclesiastes 3:1). There is a time for you to focus on your life—to learn your likes, your dislikes, and your God-given gifts and talents. *Now* is that time. Don't feel guilty; this is going to be a healthy self-evaluation with a purpose. My prayer for you, dear reader, is that by the time you're done, you will be much better acquainted with the *real you.*

Let's face it. Too many of us are preoccupied with wanting to be wanted, wanting to just *be* with someone, *anyone*, rather than being alone. Loneliness is a killer feeling—one that I have known intimately. And it can drive us to make unwise choices. But listen: it's OK to feel desperate. It's OK to admit you have those feelings. What's not OK is to allow your feelings of desperation to affect your choice in a husband.

I didn't.

I know from experience it's not easy. It takes a willful, sacrificial, conscious effort. You will have to stop wasting years dating guys who show you early on they're not the ones for you. You will have to sacrifice the comfort of being with "just anyone" in order to find the "right one." Your commitment to choose what's best for you *will* deliver an exciting and fulfilling future. So hang in there with me. You can be strong in the face of loneliness. I have faith in you; otherwise I wouldn't be spending months at my computer for you!

The fact is, you will only marry from the pool of men you date. So be picky! You've only got one life to live. From this point forward, focus on the qualities you admire in a man rather than on your gnawing inner need to be wanted. It will pay off, I promise.

To continue, you will need some supplies: a notebook or journal and a pen. Every time you pick up this book, pick up your journal too. Are you ready? Open your notebook, grab your pen, and let's get started.

EXERCISE 1: HOW DID I GET HERE?

Have you ever stopped and asked yourself, *How in the world did I get here?* I know I have—usually right after being dumped and having my heart sent through a paper shredder. What has *your* love life brought you thus far?

Let's consider the personal want ad you've been subconsciously carrying around with you in your dating life. Open your journal. Use one page for each dating relationship you've had. Put each ex-boyfriend's name at the top of a page and then draw a line down the middle. On one side of the page, write all of this person's good qualities; on the other side, write all of his bad qualities. Do this for each guy you've gone out with. Some of you may need only one or two pages; others may need to buy a second notebook.

Come on now, I heard that! Each of your ex-boyfriends had at least *one* good quality, or you wouldn't have dated him in the first place! Did he take you out to dinner, open the door for you, go to church, have a job, feed his pets, clean his bathroom? He must have had a redeeming characteristic hidden *somewhere.* Go ahead and write anything that comes to mind, good or bad.

After you've completed your lists, go back and circle every negative and positive quality that is repeated in at least two of your guys. Cross out everything else. Finished? OK, now make a new list of all the positive qualities you've circled, and pat yourself on the back for doing something right in your dating life. (Some of the positives that tended to repeat in my ex-boyfriends included "attractive," "employed," "churchgoing," "athletic," and "popular.")

Next, I want you to set aside your positive list and write a personal ad for a man based on the *negative* qualities you've circled. I hope you will be able to laugh out loud when you read your ad! I sure laughed at mine. Here it is:

WANTED: Angry, irresponsible victim from unstable, alcoholic, abusive family. Must be self-absorbed and critical of every move I make. If I have a blemish, you must point it out—especially if your past girlfriend was a flawless beauty. I'll be hooked if you keep me feeling I'm not good enough for you. As long as I feel I'll lose you at any moment, I'll stay in love, especially if you discount my feelings and withhold love from me. Obsessing on a past relationship is a plus, as well as being bitter about your childhood. If you blame everyone but yourself for your unhappiness, then I'm the one for you.

I was shocked! Why was I attracting these qualities from nearly every guy I dated? All but one came from a broken family. Most had histories of abuse of some sort and at least one alcoholic parent. Tragically, two had fathers whose drinking was responsible for someone else's death. Yikes! Though all my ex-boyfriends looked very different from one another on the outside and had diverse interests and careers—they included a pro golfer, a pilot, a businessman, a fireman, a cop, a concert promoter, a producer, a model, an actor, a singer, and a financial planner, among others—they all were really the same. They were wounded and needed me. Or so I thought.

Apparently I was in the habit of subconsciously looking for a man in need. Not that all of us don't have some degree of brokenness in our lives; but if a man needed me to fix him, I falsely believed that rescuing him would make him fall deeply in love with me. Wrong! Every man I "fixed" soon left me for another woman. Ouch!

I wised up and realized that something or someone had to change. Since I was the only person I could control, I decided I was the one I'd work on. As I became aware of my personal dating patterns, I began to choose my dates more wisely. I still experienced a good deal of heartbreak before Mr. Right appeared. But since I had begun choosing to be with men whose positive qualities I admired— and to avoid those men whose negative qualities spelled trouble— my relationships were often shorter but closer to my dream.

When I first started dating my husband, Will, I have to admit I just couldn't figure out what he saw in me. He didn't need me to fix anything for him. He didn't want me to make him a star. He didn't need my help guiding his career. He didn't need me to puff up his ego or change his hairstyle. Wow, dating a nonneedy guy was a first for me! And boy, did it feel great!

MR. PERSONALITY

In the spring of 2003, the Fox Network began airing one of its many reality dating series. This short-lived one was called *Mr. Personality.* A bachelorette chose a potential husband from twenty-five masked men. She didn't get to see what a particular suitor looked like until she had either eliminated him or chosen him at last as the one to keep. I was so intrigued by the premise that I just had to watch the show. Based on the ratings, many other people in America were dying to know if a woman could pick a good mate without ever seeing his face.

During the brief series some of the handsome male contestants' comments were quite ridiculous and downright nervy. Because the gal couldn't see their faces, she took seriously some of the things they said—things she might have laughed off as a joke in a normal dating environment. But because she wasn't distracted by their looks, she quickly eliminated these misbehaving contestants.

Oh, if that would only happen in all our dating lives! If only we could allow ourselves to see the real person underneath rather than being so mesmerized by the fireworks of physical attraction that blind us to blatant character flaws! Hopefully, this first exercise has underscored the fact that attraction by itself is a poor criteria for choosing a mate because it tends to draw us to men we would otherwise run from if we could see what's inside.

Trust me. I have wasted so much time in my life dating guys who were gorgeous on the outside and absolutely scary on the inside! I was attracted to the scrumptious pretty boys—you know, the model types you see in magazines. But few had the character of a man worth keeping. Don't get me wrong; there's nothing wrong with a beautiful man. Show me a hunk with good character any day, and we're in business! I was just having trouble tracking one of those down. Being attracted to your man is obviously very important. But equally important, if not more so, is being attracted to his character and personality.

The pitter-patter head-swirl of new love is a chemical reaction, not a guarantee of lifelong passion. If you will just remember that, you will save yourself a whole lot of heartache in the long run. You *will be* physically attracted to men who are very wrong for you. Their outsides will look good, but their personalities, backgrounds, values, likes, and dislikes will be all wrong. So vow to yourself that from here on out, you'll start paying attention to what you are getting from the inside out.

EXERCISE 2: A MAN WORTH KEEPING

Now that you know what you've *been* getting, it's time to confess your heart's secret desire and design your very own Prince Charming. In this second exercise, you're going to write a personal ad for a man worth keeping. This may be difficult at first, since many of us find it easier to gripe about what we don't have and complain about what we do have than clarify, even to ourselves, what we truly want. Today we will change that.

Don't worry about what others might think if they were to read your ad. It's for your eyes only at this point. And don't write what you think *someone else* wants for you. What others want for you and what you want for yourself may be totally different. Just write what you would want if you could have any man in the world. Besides, you're a woman; you can always change your mind later!

Open your journal to the next blank page and write "A Man Worth Keeping" at the top. Then go crazy and have fun writing out your fairy tale. Allow yourself the freedom to be ridiculous. If you have a dream of being swept off your feet, write that down. If you want a knight in shining armor to come galloping in on horseback, write it down. There's power in the pen. A few years ago, after a Sunday church service in Bel Air, California, a girlfriend of mine was literally swept off her feet. Her boyfriend dressed up as a knight in shining armor and came galloping up the church driveway to propose in front of the whole congregation. So you just never know!

Ten Questions to Ask

Search your heart and write out what you really want in a man. Be general at first, and then get specific with your answers to these questions:

1. What character qualities do you want in a husband?

2. Where will you live?

3. How many kids will you have?

4. How will you serve God together? Will you have the same beliefs? Does it matter which church denomination you attend? How involved will you both be in church?

5. What can you not live without?

6. How will you handle money together?

7. How will you spend your leisure time together, and how often will you do these things?

8. What will his career and work schedule be like? Will you both work outside the home?

9. Is it OK if he's been married before? What if he has children from a previous relationship?

10. What will he look like physically?

Time to Get Specific

Now take the answers to the previous questions and go deeper. Which answers represent nonnegotiable "must-haves," and which ones are more flexible?

Get very specific. If you wrote that you're looking for a "funny Christian guy with a job," do you mean Jim Carey–funny or Bill Cosby–funny? By "Christian," do you mean an Easter/Christmas Christian, a Sundays-only Christian, or a believer who lives a devout Christian life seven days a week? By "job," do you mean *any* job? Does it matter how long he's had it? If he's often in and out of work? If he hates what he does? These are the kinds of questions that can help you really focus on the details of your dream man.

Now go to the next blank page of your journal and write at the top, "My Husband." Put today's date next to it. Then, pulling everything together from your lists and answers thus far, write a personal ad or "husband wish list" for a man who, in your estimation, is worth keeping forever. It can be a paragraph or a page. Here's how my personal ad read from June 14, 1992, until my wedding day.

My Husband
Last Revision: June 14, 1992

My man knows he wants me and actively pursues me—he does the chasing while I encourage him. He treats me like a lady and like a prize he's won. He treats me as though he's proud to be with me, and I do the same for him.

My man is a man of God—a Christian who is as interested in serving God as I am. He is involved or willing to be involved in our home church. He tithes. He is in control of his finances and willing to talk about it and learn even more. He is financially at a level equal or greater than my own. He is more on the conservative side of things but likes adventure. He is generous with his money but not foolish.

We are both confident with our own lives and have strong self-esteem. He is a true man who knows what he wants in his life and is motivated and dedicated to achieving his goals. He is open to pre-marital counseling. He has male friends, and I keep my girlfriends. We have friends together as well, and we throw barbecues, etc.

We play together and have fun with our free time. We do things together—building furniture, working on home improvements, hiking, traveling, lounging in the Jacuzzi, going to church, cooking, dining, going to movies and concerts, etc.

We can talk—in fact, we could just sit and talk for hours about life, problems, plans, solutions, faith, money. He is the spiritual leader of the house. I love his voice and listening to him reason. I love to lean on him and he on me. I feel safe being vulnerable with him and he with me.

He is dedicated to me and I to him. He works through any problems we have. He is loyal, and he thinks I'm the best woman to ever come into his life. He cherishes me, and I gladly respect, admire, and nourish him.

He may be a speaker. He is a successful businessman from a good family. He lives in Los Angeles County or Orange County. My family likes him and feels comfortable around him. He is no more than five years older than me. He is gorgeous to me (but not a pretty boy) and has a good build. He is about six feet tall and 175 pounds. He has brunette hair possibly. He has no children from a previous marriage and wants to have kids. And he's open to me having a live-in maid/childcare. We have Bible study with our kids. He doesn't let our kids be spoiled. He believes in discipline with love (spanking).

From the day I wrote it, I kept this personal husband wish list as the opening page of my day planner and carried it everywhere I went until my wedding day. OK, so I was a bit obsessed, but it worked! My eventual husband met every single condition on my list except two—he lived significantly farther than fifty miles away (across the country, in fact), and I don't have a live-in maid . . . yet. But I'm living happily ever after anyway.

A LIST FOR YOUR FRIENDS

Now that you have an ad or wish list for your eyes only, turn it into an easy-to-remember paragraph or a series of descriptive words or statements you can share with anyone who asks what you're looking for in a date. I used to tell folks I was looking for the Five Ss: single, sexy, successful, saved, and sane.

Here's what I meant:

1. *Single.* Any man I dated had to be single. I don't believe in ever going out with a married man—you will never win that way. Even if you ignore the fact that it's adultery, please hear me on this point: if he will cheat on his wife to go out with you, he will one day cheat on you. A cheater is always a cheater, period.

2. *Sexy.* If I wasn't attracted to him, then I wouldn't be able to kiss him. My rule of thumb, was if I couldn't bring myself to kiss a guy by the fifth date, I moved on.

3. *Successful.* I knew I needed a man who had direction in his life—one with a career he was proud of. To me, a successful man is a respectable, responsible citizen who pays his taxes

and his bills on time. He is a man who works for a living and enjoys it. I can respect a man like that. And respect is crucial!

4. *Saved.* I am a Christian, and my personal relationship with Jesus Christ is the most important relationship in my life. Any man I married would need to share my faith.

5. *Sane.* This is self-explanatory. I was looking for someone stable and nonabusive verbally or physically, a man who wasn't on drugs and didn't drink too much. Life's too short to settle for less.

Play with *your* list and come up with your own slogan or catch phrase so you'll never be at a loss for words when someone asks you what you're looking for in a man. If you can't think of something of your own, feel free to use my Five Ss. I'd be honored!

LET THE SECRETS WORK FOR YOU

There now. You've just completed two exercises that have (1) exposed what you've been getting thus far in your love life and (2) helped you pinpoint what you really want in a mate. Do you feel empowered already? By merely doing these two simple yet crucial activities, you are well on the way to breaking old patterns that weren't working for you. Congratulate yourself! You now know what a man worth keeping looks like. You have set yourself on a path toward a marriage that will last. I'm so proud that you love yourself enough to put in the time and effort to design your own bright future.

Don't stop now. This is only the beginning. I waited a long time to find Mr. Right. In the process I was willing to be lonely and alone rather than lonely and in the wrong relationship. (If you've already been married and divorced, you know how crucial it is to make that decision.) And God came through for me big time!

I know he will come through for you too.

Am I saying that virtually every single gal who reads this book will get married? No, I'm not. What I am saying is this: if you follow my ten dating secrets with persistence and passion, beginning with these first two exercises, you will find out quite vividly who you are and what you want. You will be empowered to pursue the life you've always wanted. You will avoid or escape dangerous relationships, reduce the number of heartbreaks in your future, and either find a fabulous husband or notice that God is lessening and maybe even eliminating your desire for marriage.

Yes, some of us are meant to be single. But I truly believe that God ultimately gives us the desires of our heart. Therefore, I encourage you to hang in there and persevere if your desire for marriage does not go away. Follow my secrets and wait on God's timing. As my father often said throughout my childhood, "Nothing worthwhile comes easy."

So go ahead. Write your husband wish list. Look at it daily and pray over it constantly. Feel free to modify it when you feel certain that something should be added or deleted. But be absolutely committed to your nonnegotiables. If you're willing to stick to your list, either the man you find will be worth the wait, or you'll be far better off staying single!

T U R N
Y O U R
L I F E
Inside Out

I hopped on a plane with two girlfriends to ease my latest heartbreak. A week before Christmas, I had been dumped by a guy who was now going to marry a new girlfriend in May. I didn't just go across state lines to mourn. I flew across the world, to the French Alps.

For many years fear had stopped me from pursuing much of what I wanted. Now I was in France, in desperate need of change. Terrified of heights, I marveled at the crazy people I saw floating in the sky with their kitelike parasails, appearing to be the size of butterflies. Each of them had leaped off the twelve-thousand-foot mountain my friends and I had descended the day before.

To this day I don't know why I let my girlfriend talk me into paying the money to tandem jump with an instructor. Maybe it was because I needed to do something drastic. Maybe I needed to turn my life inside out, face my fears, and start anew. Whatever the reason, once paid, there was no refund. So we just did it. My friend first, then an hour later, me. Attached to the instructor, I ran right off that mountain; forty-five minutes later, I gratefully kissed the ground. Did I love parasailing? No, I hated every moment. *But I did it.* I faced my fear, took the leap, and changed my life. Since that day, whenever I confront a terrifying obstacle, I remember, *Hey, I jumped off a twelve-thousand-foot mountain. I can face this.*

By now you know what you want in a husband. Yet here you are, seemingly stuck in the husband waiting game. I assume Mr. Everything has yet to appear on your doorstep. Or at least he hasn't placed that beautiful solitaire on your third finger. Either way, I'd venture to say you're ready to see a change in your life—something, somehow, somewhere.

So maybe you won't mind my asking: considering the gap between what you've been getting and what you're looking for, are *you* marriage material?

Wow, that's a bold question! You may want to throw down this book right now and say, "How rude, shallow, and prejudiced! Everyone is datable!"

Hang in there with me. To catch a man worth keeping, you need to be a prize worth winning. And a woman worth winning is, first of all, *intriguing*. At this very moment in your life, would you say you are intriguing? Or are you more, shall we say, boring?

TELL ME WHAT YOU'VE GOT

I meet ladies all the time who are so desperate to end the waiting game that they spend every waking moment yearning for a husband while putting their own lives on hold. Not only does this make them boring, it also puts too much pressure on each and every date. The entire future seems to ride on each date's success or failure.

If you've found yourself caught up in this vicious cycle, fear not. You can jump off the desperation treadmill simply by changing your perspective on single life. This requires a change in your thoughts and attitudes. Instead of wasting valuable time allowing your thoughts to focus on what you don't have, worrying that a spouse will never appear, start focusing on becoming a person worth finding!

Let's take a step in that direction right now. Pull out your journal and answer the following questions as quickly and as honestly as you can. Don't be modest. Your journal is for your eyes only, so be real:

1. What do you have to offer a spouse?

2. What are your good qualities?

3. What do you just love about yourself?

4. What favors do people usually ask of you?

5. What do your family and friends say is the driving force in your life?

6. What is unique about your background, hobbies, experiences, interests, or skills?

7. Do you think God created you for any special purpose? If so, what?

If after answering these questions you suspect you may be boring, don't panic. You can change that. Everyone can be fascinating *if* they choose to live their lives to the fullest. Does that mean you have to become an international success, a major overachiever, or a world traveler? Not if those things aren't appealing to you. Just do something, *anything*, other than sitting at home daydreaming about a man.

So, girlfriend, if you've allowed yourself to believe that the single years are a drag, snap out of it! There is no freer time in your life than right now. No matter who you think is manipulating you like a marionette—your family, your friends, your boss, your coworkers— you're actually quite free. No one will affect your comings and goings more than your future spouse. Adult singlehood is the only time in life when you get to make your own choices without having to consult someone else. At this very moment, you have the freedom to dream about being all you can be and doing all you can do. And you can pursue those cherished dreams with all your heart, time, money, and strength without feeling guilty about depriving a spouse or a child of love and attention.

Once the ring is on your finger, however, you give up sole ownership of your life. Gone are the days of leaving the house without permission. Ironically, many teens spend their high-school years dreaming of their day of freedom, when they no longer have to ask Mom and Dad's permission to go and to do. Yet many of them rush right out to find a spouse the minute they graduate and give up that hard-won privilege.

Understand, I passionately believe there are wonderful perks that go along with the merging of two lives in marriage. But I also believe you shouldn't downplay or ignore the great perk you have right now: your ability to do whatever you want anytime you want! Enjoy your freedom while it lasts so you'll be ready to completely and willingly give it up later with no "if-only" regrets. It's better to be single and alone than to be stuck in a rushed, lonely marriage, thinking about what might have been.

The fact is, what you do in your single life enables you to eventually have the married life you want. So take the leap and turn your life inside out. Appreciate every season of your life—including your single life—and start to live deliberately. If you take the risk and pursue all you dream to be and do, you will put yourself in a position to attract all you dream of finding.

THE DESIRES OF YOUR HEART

I'm going to ask you to do a lot of soul-searching as I share secret 2. In this next exercise I want you to look at your cherished hopes and dreams—even those you assume will never come to pass. This is important, so prepare to take as much time as you need. Using the next empty page in your journal, look deep into the secret corner of your heart and write a letter to yourself admitting your greatest longings and desires. Use these questions as a guide:

1. Do you have a secret dream?

2. What do you really want, even if it seems impossible to have or achieve?

3. If you could be or do anything in the world, what would that be?

4. What would being or doing that thing mean to you? What would the result or payoff be in your life?

5. Would others be blessed if you achieved this dream?

6. Would God be honored if you became this person?

Now go back and look over the letter you just wrote. If your answer to the last two questions was yes, do you have any legitimate reason not to pursue your dream? Has someone or some circumstance squashed your enthusiasm for chasing that dream? Choose today to turn off that dream-crushing voice you keep hearing in your head—no matter whose voice it is—and decide to go for it! Not only will you embark on a wonderful adventure, you will find yourself becoming fascinating to men. You see, if you actively pursue worthwhile goals while you are stuck in the waiting game, you *will* become intriguing. It's inevitable.

TO LOVE ME OR LOVE ME NOT

Recently, my husband and I attended a wedding of a close friend. It was a quaint, outdoor garden wedding at the edge of a trickling river. Surrounded by family and friends, the starry-eyed couple read beautiful, self-written vows. Everything was perfect. Still, my husband and I left the happy occasion with heavy hearts. This precious couple has so much going for them, including a deep love for one another, but we fear that their foundation is shaky. According to the vows the bride read, she'd spent all her life looking for someone, anyone, to make her happy. Now, for the first time, she felt that elusive happiness had arrived. She just knew that with her groom at her side, she would always be content.

The problem is, if she is depending exclusively on her new husband to keep her feeling of bliss alive, both newlyweds will soon be disappointed. The groom is a great guy. We know him well. But we're all human. Life happens. Crises come, and crises go.

Eventually, everyone lets down the person they love the most.

This beautiful young bride is not unique in her expectations. Sadly, the reason many women yearn so desperately for a husband is because they are subconsciously looking for someone or something— anything—to fix their inner pain. If you don't want to be disappointed in marriage, you need to embrace a very important reality: *a man is not going to make you happy.* If you are unhappy, finding a man is not going to be the pill that fixes everything. He may bring temporary symptom relief, but he is not the cure. When the medicine wears off, the reality and the pain will set back in.

Believe me, if you aren't happy in your own skin, you won't be happy merging with someone else. Because wherever you go, there you are. You can't escape you. Even if you find your man worth keeping, until you face your past—whatever it is—and learn to love yourself, you won't believe you deserve him. Somehow you will find a way to blow it. Either you'll scare him away, or you'll talk yourself out of liking him over something silly.

To find and *keep* a man worth keeping, you need to be a woman who actually loves herself. Now, that's not something that's shouted every day over the airwaves. But it's mandatory if you want to find happiness. It's not vain to love yourself. It's not selfish or rude. It's healthy, and it's biblical! In Matthew 22:39, Jesus said that you must love your neighbor "as you love yourself" (NLV). He called this the second and greatest commandment. Even non-Christians are familiar with these famous words. The fact is, if you don't love yourself, you will not make a good spouse, because you won't have the capacity to love. To love someone else, you must first learn how to love yourself.

Two halves make a whole only in mathematics, pizzas, and apple pies. In relationships it takes two whole people to make one complete and happy unit. Are you whole by yourself? Or are you broken in pieces? Of course, we all have some brokenness inside. But do you feel so broken that the pursuit of happiness seems an elusive dream that can only be realized with another person by your side? If this describes your heart right now, then a husband is not what you are searching for. You are searching for God. Only he can fill that void in your heart.

God wrote these words for you: "'For I know the plans I have for you,' declares the LORD, 'plans to prosper you and not to harm you, plans to give you hope and a future'" (Jeremiah 29:11). You were created with a purpose. As pastor Rick Warren likes to say, "We were made to have meaning!"[1] God has a plan for you—a good plan. And he is ready, willing, and able to give you hope and a great future.

Of course, not all of us were raised in nurturing homes with parents who taught us that we mattered—to God or to anyone else. If you missed that message in your upbringing, Jesus wants to heal your pain. One of the most treasured chapters in the Bible for me is Psalm 139. In this beautiful passage, King David explains that God created your innermost being. He knit you together in your mother's womb. You have been fearfully and wonderfully made—just the way you are!

More than that, God knew every day you would live and every word you would speak, not only before the thought was in your head, but before the day you were born. He even knows, at this very moment, the number of hairs on your head.[2] If God, who created this vast universe, loves you so much that he counts every hair on your head and records your every word, clearly he believes you are lovable. There is no question about it. Accept the truth!

Life is Like a Box of chocolates

One of the great blessings of my life—in hindsight, of course—was being an ugly duckling in my early years. Feeling ugly and unnoticed motivated me to develop my inner character and beauty, eventually enabling me to emerge a swan.

The fact is, who we truly are is what's found on the inside, not what's seen on the outside. It's like a box of chocolates you receive at Easter or on Valentine's Day. Every one of those tiny chocolate morsels looks enticing when you first open the box, but when you take a bite—"Oh, yuk, that's not what I expected!" Most get returned to the box, partially eaten and totally rejected. What's my point? If we don't work on our insides—the hidden gooey centers—we'll continue being the rejected pieces of chocolate, enticing for a moment but ultimately discarded.

Have you stopped to look inside yourself lately? Too often we let busy schedules—school, work, community service, church—cover up who we really are. We use our busyness as an excuse to ignore our dreams and the changes we may need to make in order to achieve them. Instead, we live our lives day in and day out, allowing our habits, pasts, and unconscious thoughts to determine our fate. We get up, put on our clothes, and go to school or work. If we have jobs, it's because we fell into them as a means to pay the bills. We walk through life with blinders on, allowing our girlish dreams to fall by the wayside.

It doesn't have to be that way. You can change your life today. No matter how old you are or what you've experienced in the past, you can start fresh. It's not over unless you give up!

I Remember the Time . . .

Ah, to be young again, before disappointment, rejection, and discouragement tarnished your world-view! Do you remember a time when your life was carefree? What were your dreams for the future *then*? Sure, plans change as we grow, but many times our hopes and dreams don't change; they just hide.

Here's something you need to know: Many of your dreams were placed in your heart by God himself. If they've been lost, they can be found again! That's why I want you to take on a big assignment: I want you to think back over your life and write down your life story in your journal—an autobiography of sorts. Now, don't get overwhelmed. You don't have to do it all in one sitting. And you don't have to write fifty pages. Who knows, you may fall in love with the process and begin writing your own book! But for now, just start scribbling down memories as they come.

Do you have old diaries, photos, yearbooks, or scrapbooks you can pull out? Reading the notes in yearbooks are great memory triggers for fledgling dreams. By going into your attic of yesteryear, you just may dig out your blueprint for tomorrow.

To help get your thoughts flowing, jot down the following titles on a few journal pages: "Birth through Age Five," "Elementary School," "Junior High/Middle School," "High School," "Eighteen to Twenty-One/College Years," "Twenties," "Thirties" (keep adding decades if you qualify). Then answer the following questions for each age group:

1. Where did you live?

2. Who were your friends and enemies?

3. What did you do?

4. What were your dreams and future plans at this stage in your life?

5. How did you view God, and what role did God play in your life at that time?

6. What were some of the blessings and victories you experienced?

7. What were some of your biggest disappointments and hurts?

Though tedious, this exercise is worth the effort, even if it takes you a month of daily writing to complete it. No matter where you've been, it's healthy to stop and reflect on the triumphs and the tragedies, the hurts and the joys, the mistakes and the right moves you've made in your life. Collectively, these events have played a major role in molding you into who you are. So keep plugging away until you've exhausted all the questions for each age group.

When you're finally done, skim back over the pages. Did you see any common themes running through the age groups? Did you have any "aha!" moments, when something about your life suddenly made sense to you? Here are a few more questions:

1. Do any plans, goals, or dreams recur across age groups?

2. Which of those dreams and desires are still in your heart today?

3. Do any of the dreams in these pages coincide with the desires of your heart from the previous exercise?

4. What could you do today to take a step toward turning your dreams into reality?

knock off the ol' block

Some time ago I set up my pretty, smart, and successful girlfriend, Carol, with one of my handsome, successful, funny buddies, Steve. I hoped it would be a match made in heaven. Shortly after their date, I got the update from Steve.

"Carol was all you said she was, Victorya, but she just bugged me," he said. When I asked why, he stated simply, "She is one of the most negative and sarcastic people I've ever met."

I was so bummed! You see, Carol isn't really like that. Sure, she can be sarcastic at times, but negative is not how I would describe her. Apparently, at that point in her life, she had been so hurt and disappointed by men that she couldn't go on a date and hold back her biting tongue.

As you look back over your autobiography, do you notice that perhaps you, too, have a chip on your shoulder? Are those feelings causing you to be sarcastic, pessimistic, or downright cranky? Here's the rub: Who we are is, in large part, an accumulation of everything that has happened to us thus far in our lives. And most of us have been hurt not once, not twice, but many times. But no matter how unjust the pain or how innocent we were in the wrongdoing, we were, and still are, responsible for our response to our circumstances. Our reactions play a major role in molding us into who we become.

That said, I urge you to make it a priority to work on healing your hurts. There is no shame in seeking help, which is readily available through a variety of sources. You can start by visiting the self-help section of your local bookstore, library, or online e-store (such as www.amazon.com or www.christianbook.com) and reading books that focus on healing your area of hurt. (A few great ones include any of the books in the Boundaries series by Henry Cloud and John Townsend, *Have You Felt Like Giving Up Lately?* by David Wilkerson, *Codependent No More: How to Stop Controlling Others and Start Caring for Yourself* by Melody Beattie, and *People of the Lie: The Hope for Healing Human Evil* by M. Scott Peck.)

If you need to go further, counseling is available through many churches and is either free or inexpensive. You can also find a Christian counselor in your area by searching through referral Web sites such as:

- www.newlife.com (New Life Ministries)
- www.crosssearch.com/health/counseling (a ministry of Gospelcom.net)
- www.aacc.net (American Association of Christian Counselors)
- www.nanc.org/counselors/index.php (The National Association of Nouthetic Counselors)

Getting healed emotionally is crucial to attaining your dream of finding a man worth keeping. If your self-esteem has been demolished by people or circumstances in the past, when Mr. Wonderful shows up, you will either sabotage the relationship or ignore his advances because you feel unworthy.

If you've been single a long time and have been disappointed over and over again in relationships, you may have a chip on your shoulder (like Carol did) that is noticeable to everyone but yourself. If that's the case, please realize that your past failures are not the fault of your future relationships. So why punish your potential mate-to-be?

I am in no way discounting the depth of pain you may have experienced. But at the risk of sounding harsh, I have to tell you frankly: face it, fix it, and yes, willfully choose to get over it—whatever "it" is. You have to heal your hurts and lose your anger and bitterness if you want to be a prize worth winning.

"But, Victorya, you don't know what I've been through. You don't know how abused I was or how hurt I am." No, I don't know your story. But I do know that whatever has happened, whatever the hurt, God is big enough to heal it. In Matthew 11:28–30, Jesus said, "Come to me, all you who are weary and burdened, and I will give you rest. Take my yoke upon you and learn from me, for I am gentle and humble in heart, and you will find rest for your souls. For my yoke is easy and my burden is light." Unrelenting anger, bitterness, and desire for revenge will destroy your future happiness. Choose to let it go. Believe me, if you are bitter and sour, you will not attract the positive result you yearn for. Forgiving and letting go is tough but mandatory if you want to eventually have a healthy relationship with a wonderful husband.

GET A LIFE

I love this quote from Bruce Wilkinson's book *Dream Giver*: "Every Nobody was made to be a Somebody."[3] I think *Dream Giver* is a must-read for every Christian—especially single Christians. Through a compelling modern-day parable, Wilkinson tells the tale of Ordinary, who dares to leave the Land of Familiar to pursue his Big Dream. And we all have a big dream, don't we? Wilkinson's fable inspires us to keep moving toward that dream, no matter what roadblocks we may encounter.

Now is the time to get a life—beginning right where you are. And here's the first step: *be prepared to be single forever.*

Wait a minute! I know your heart is probably palpitating at such a horrible thought. Stop. Take a moment. Breathe in. Breathe out. As we said in the first secret, some women may not get married, and if that's God's plan for them, that's OK. He will make it OK. I'm not saying you're going to be one of them (although you might be). What I am saying is, the fear of that possibility may be what's keeping you from preparing yourself for Mr. Right. And that same fear may be what will keep you from recognizing him when he shows up at your door.

There are no "do-overs" in life. Each precious twenty-four-hour day goes by so fast! So don't waste your time pining away about what could be. You just can't afford to waste another day!

Instead, hang in there. Prepare for and begin living a vital single life, because right now you *are* single. That doesn't mean you're giving up hope for finding a marriage partner. It just means you're deciding to "get a life" *today*. What are your passions, your goals, your ambitions, your hobbies, your career dreams? Those are the things you need to explore.

During my single years, I didn't know what my future held, but God did. Looking back, I can see that through every experience, every relationship, and yes, every heartbreak, he was purposefully preparing me for the life I have today. Now I have everything I dreamed of when I was younger: a wonderful, dreamboat husband, two precious children, and a speaking career that takes me around the country.

Wow, who would have thought I would ever be worthy of all that? Of course, I'm not worthy; I'm just loved by God. So are you. That's how precious our heavenly Father is. I'm convinced that God put those dreams in my heart way back during my Barbie-doll and fairy-tale days. And I'm convinced that as I grew older, God directed my path through each hopeful romance and teary breakup. Ultimately the fulfillment of my dreams came in God's perfect timing.

I'm no more important to Jesus than you are. That's why I know God has placed personalized dreams in your heart, too, that he intends to fulfill. Proverbs 3:5–6 says, "Trust in the LORD with all your heart; do not depend on your own understanding. Seek his will in all you do, and he will direct your paths" (NLT). Just as he did for me, God will direct your steps and fulfill your dreams in his own perfect timing, if you will allow him to. Believe it!

The Life You Always Wanted

Once again, pull out your journal and answer these questions:

1. What have you been telling yourself you'll achieve after you get married?

2. What are your dreams and goals for:

- Your education and career

- Your relationships

- Travel and leisure opportunities

- Your spiritual life

- Your home

- Your life accomplishments

With these answers fresh in your mind, turn the page in your journal and spend the next five minutes writing anything and everything that comes to mind about what you want to be and do in this life. Don't edit as you write; just keep your pen moving freely.

Next, look over what you've just written. Pray for God's will and guidance over these dreams and goals and commit to taking active steps to pursue them. What are you passionate about? Pursue *that*. You will end up attracting someone who is fascinated by that passion! Of course, if you don't pursue any goals, you'll still get somewhere—just not anywhere you want to go. So why not go after what you really want, so you can live the life you've always wanted? Don't you want to be able to sit in a rocking chair in your old age and reminisce on a life well lived rather than find yourself mourning a life filled with regrets?

A Life Well Lived?

As you know, I graduated from high school without a boyfriend and spent the next four years chasing my MRS degree. But instead of becoming a "Mrs." I ended up with a BA in journalism. Since dating didn't seem to be getting me anywhere, I focused on my career. I broke into the entertainment field, worked my way up the ladder, and became a talent agent in Beverly Hills, representing some amazing people in television and film for more than a decade.

Successful? Yes, by certain standards. But the fulfillment of many of my dreams was nowhere in sight. In many ways I was sleepwalking through life. By the age of twenty-five, however, I finally woke up. God opened my eyes through much searching, prayer, a Bible study on God's grace (Chuck Swindoll's *Grace Awakening*), and a particular Scripture passage, Ephesians 2:8–9: "For it is by grace you have been saved, through faith—and this not from yourselves, it is the gift of God—not by works, so that no one can boast."

I came to understand that Jesus not only loved me, he also had a special, personalized plan for my life. I claimed the promise of John 10:10—that Jesus came to give me life, and life abundantly! And I chose to begin living abundantly every day.

So in my midtwenties, with no man in sight, I decided that I would simply enjoy the moments of my life. Two girlfriends joined me, and we got into hiking, rollerblading, and the great outdoors. Once a month we visited a tourist trap, whether a museum or an amusement park. Once a month we went to the mountains for the weekend. And once a year we traveled someplace outside our state—preferably outside the country. What great adventures we had! We had to scrimp and save, but our experiences were worth the sacrifice.

I traveled much of the world, bought a condo, had a career, developed lasting friendships, obtained two college degrees, paid off debts, set up a retirement fund, and so much more. In that process I never stopped looking for my husband. But now I can say that I did it all. I even parasailed off that twelve-thousand-foot mountain in the French Alps! I learned to enjoy the moments of my life while searching for my mate.

Newsflash: you, too, can be stuck in the waiting game and still live life with flair and a genuine smile. You can chase your dreams. You can pursue an education and a great career. You can see the world.

I mean, think about it: if you could travel anywhere in the world, and money wasn't a problem, where would you go? I've heard every excuse in the book for not leaving home, including, "Oh, I want to save those memories for my spouse." Life is too short to wait for the unknown future to arrive! Besides, you can always play tour guide if your spouse hasn't been to the places you have. How fun would that be?

Yes, traveling can be expensive. But there are also many bargains out there. Shop the Internet for your airfare, hotel, and car rentals. A few of my favorite discount travel Web sites include:

- www.expedia.com
- www.cheaptrips.com
- www.orbitz.com

Check your weekend newspaper for travel packages. And if you have the luxury of being flexible on your vacation time and location, be impulsive and plan your trip at the last minute. You'll get the best savings, especially on cruises and at all-inclusive resorts that have spaces available.

Get a Grip on Your Money

Another thing you can do while you're single is learn how to manage your money *before* you're in a position to have to share it. When

I was single, I decided to buy a condo. At the time, however, I was more than $25,000 in credit-card debt, with eighteen high-interest credit cards in my wallet. Yikes! I finally came to the realization that if I wanted to buy a home, not to mention attract a spouse, I had to get a grip on my money, put a halt to my overspending, and get out of debt. Since then I've become a big fan of financial consultants Larry Burkett and Mary Hunt. Within three years of studying their books, I was able to get out and stay out of debt. I cut up all but two low-interest credit cards and committed myself to paying them off each month. I kept my MasterCard for the frequent flyer miles.

Few people stop to think how important it is to have financial health. Did you know that sixteen of the thirty-eight parables Jesus told have to do with handling money and possessions? Indeed, Jesus said more about money than about almost any other subject. The Bible offers 500 verses on prayer, fewer than 500 verses on faith, but more than 2,350 verses on money and possessions.[4] Hebrews 13:5 is just one of them: "Keep your lives free from the love of money and be content with what you have, because God has said, 'Never will I leave you; never will I forsake you.'" If God cares about such things, shouldn't we?

We need to wake up and face the bank statement! Financial stress is always at or near the top of the list of reasons experts give for marriage failure. If you really want to get married and stay married, you can't afford to overlook this area of your life. Don't you think it would be wise to get a grip on the money monster now, when you're the only one being affected?

Let's stop for a reality check. Are you handling your money well? Are you giving a portion of your money to God's work and to help others? Are you overspending? Are you in debt? If you owe money, do everything you can to pay it back while you're single. Not many guys are anxious to take on a woman *and* her megadebt!

Take a detailed look at your financial situation. In your journal or in a budgeting notebook, write out how many credit cards you carry, how much debt you owe on each one, and what you plan to do to stop borrowing. Go out today and buy a good book on money management by a credible author such as Sharon Durling, Larry Burkett, Dave Ramsey, Randy Alcorn, or Mary Hunt. Or go to one of these Web sites:

- www.sharondurling.com

- www.crown.org (Larry Burkett's Crown Financial Ministries)

- www.daveramsey.com

- www.epm.org (Randy Alcorn's ministry)

- www.cheapskatemonthly.com (Mary Hunt's Web site)

Start today to get your financial house in order. You'll sleep better, and your future spouse will thank you for loving him enough to handle your money well.

CHANGING FOR THE RIGHT REASONS

Thirty-three-year-old Crystal has been a dog lover since she was five years old. She's a dog breeder, a frequent animal rescuer, and has three dogs of her own. Recently, she made the tough decision to break up with a new boyfriend who kept pressuring her to get rid of her dogs due to his allergies. Crystal knew that giving up dogs would be giving up her very passion. For her, it was better to lose the man early on in order to be herself, keep her passion for life, and eventually find someone who shares her love for animals.

What's my point? If anything in this chapter has inspired you to change something about yourself, do it for you, not for a man. In fact, the very best time to work on yourself is when you don't have a man in your life; that's when you have the best chance of making changes that are true to yourself and likely to last. The danger of changing for a man is that your changes will probably be temporary, and you will end up feeling like a phony "poser."

Remember, the reason for choosing to work on yourself is to love yourself. Why? We've said it before: No matter where you go, there you are. You can dump men, you can dump friends, but you're always stuck with you. If you decide to turn your life inside out, do it for the right reasons. Do it for you. Do it to become the woman God created you to be.

Live your life fully while you're in the husband waiting game. Be the person you always wanted to be but didn't think you could be. Do the things you always wanted to do but were afraid to try. Feel the fear—and do it anyway. You will make mistakes along the way. Perhaps you'll blow it some days. We all do. We're only human. But hopefully you'll learn from every mistake and grow a little more each day.

Choose to turn your life inside out. Pursue your purpose and your dreams. And before you know it, I promise, your inner swan will emerge, and you will have become a prize worth winning.

TAKE AN HONEST LOOK IN *the Mirror*

I'm from California. And in California, what God didn't grace us with, we pay for. God did not grace me with a sun-kissed, golden tan. No, I was given pearly white, ivory skin. Which was fine except during every single summer of my life.

In my late teens, I was thrilled when a product called Sudden Tan showed up in stores. Today the cosmetic companies have perfected self-tanning products, but back then they were brand-new. When Sudden Tan hit the market, I went for it. And I didn't waste any time reading the directions.

Big mistake.

Why do life lessons always seem to come to me in public? Not only was I in my first year of college, surrounded by thousands of college students—including lots of eligible men—but I was also a grocery-store checker facing hundreds of customers each day.

I purchased the self-tanner, ran home, and eagerly lathered it all over my body. During the next hour, I watched it develop into a beautiful, golden tan. So cool! But since I didn't read the instructions, I didn't realize how vitally important it was to wash my hands immediately after applying. Oops! While most of my body was turning a nice sun-kissed glow, my hands were staining deep tangerine orange with streaks up to my elbows!

What followed were five days of utter humiliation as I tried to hide my hands and arms as best I could at school and grab people's money at the grocery store without showing my palms. Talk about a challenge! Here I was, in the middle of my ugly-duckling years, and I had turned my hands and arms orange. All in the pursuit of beauty! I was so utterly horrified, I thought I would die.

Clearly, *beauty* is a relative term. Just look at the revolving door of what's "fashionable" from decade to decade and even year to year. Still, there are some aspects of beauty that are universal. Let me clue you in on a few basics that will dramatically increase your chances for attracting a man's attention—the sort of man you now know you want.

THE FIRST TIME EVER I SAW YOUR FACE

Men always seem to remember their first encounter with someone new. For some reason, good or bad, that first memory sticks with them. Therefore, how you present yourself to the world is quite relevant to becoming a woman who is a prize worth winning.

Of course, your physical appearance by itself will not sustain a relationship, but it certainly can help or hinder initiating one. What people see on the outside affects what they are willing to see on the inside. And that willingness is decided quickly. According to a study at Yale University, people make first-impression judgments within three seconds of meeting a new person.[1] Wow! To think that three seconds can determine your chance of having someone choose or not choose to get to know you!

How you look is only a small part of who you are, but it is the part that is judged first—and often most harshly. Like it or not, that's human nature. A first impression is seldom accurate, of course, but it will prevail until proven wrong.

So I have to ask, what kind of first impression are you offering a potential spouse? What about that impression is in your control, and what is outside your control? You may be surprised to find that much of how you present yourself is up to you. Every person has some beauty and some beast. The trick is to accentuate the beauty and minimize the beast. These are the things we will focus on in this chapter. We'll leave the out-of-our-control stuff to God.

To get started, I want you to pull out your journal again. Take a few moments to think about how you are perceived by the world around you versus how you want to be perceived. Answer the following questions as honestly as you can:

1. How do you think your friends describe you to potential dates? Here are a few possibilities: "Oh, she's a doll, and she has the cutest personality!" "She's a little plain, but she's such a nice girl." "She is so gorgeous (or classy, or special). You will definitely owe me for this one!"

2. How would you like to be described?

3. What needs to change in order for your friends to describe you the way you want to be perceived by the opposite sex?

4. Which of these changes are in your control?

During my teen years I dreamed of having a boy notice me. Sadly, even though many boys—even popular ones—considered me a friend, I was never the girl they wanted to date or kiss. By my twenties I was fed up with being everyone's "friend." I determined to change that perception. I set out to learn the walk, the talk, and the look that would attract a gorgeous hunk. I read every beauty book or magazine I could get my hands on. You name it, I studied it. Being a Hollywood agent working with glamorous movie stars didn't hurt either.

In the process I discovered three keys to beauty that changed everything for me. These primary elements are as important to beauty as red, blue, and yellow are to the color wheel. All other aspects of beauty spin off from them. What are these primaries? Cleanliness, a warm smile, and good posture. All three are confidence builders and mood enhancers.

Even naturally beautiful women can increase their attractiveness by applying these three keys. In the introduction I noted that Queen Esther, considered one of the most beautiful women of the ancient world, spent one year being "beautified" before she was presented to the king as a potential bride. Esther 2:12 explains: "Before a girl's turn came to go in to King Xerxes, she had to complete twelve months of beauty treatments prescribed for the women, six months with oil of myrrh and six with perfumes and cosmetics." Wouldn't it be nice if we all got such pampering and assistance! The fact is, even the most beautiful among us have to work at looking our best.

clean up your act

The first key to beauty is cleanliness. It's amazing how something as basic as a splash of water and a dab of deodorant can greatly increase your chances for finding a good husband. We are no longer in the Elizabethan era, where bathing once a month was socially acceptable! These days any of the following can be a turnoff to a man worth keeping:

- Dirty fingernails
- Dirty hair
- Dirty teeth
- A messy car
- A messy home
- Messy clothes
- Dirty or messy *anything*

Get in the habit of bathing or showering daily. If you hate to wash your hair that often, you can always wear a shower cap. Personally I am a die-hard for washing my hair every day, even though most hairdressers will tell you that every other day is better. I think my hair looks greasy when I don't wash it. But you need to decide what looks best and is healthiest for your own hair.

Make sure your nails are clean, filed, and brushed with a solid coat of nail polish. Use a clear polish if you prefer. Ragged nails and chipped polish give the impression that you don't care about your appearance.

Wear light makeup that best matches your skin color. Choose blush, eye shadow, and lip colors that are natural and complement your skin—not loud, dark colors that may confuse you with a circus clown. If you need help or want a new look, go to the makeup counter at the nearest major department store and ask for a free makeover. The sales gal will gladly try out her products on you in hopes that you'll purchase her skin-care line.

A girlfriend of mine who battles depression says that one of her first signs of an oncoming bout is the feeling of not wanting to get out of bed in the morning. On those days she is in no mood to dress, shower, or start her day. But when she forces herself to get up, take a shower, and get dressed anyway, she feels much better.

Can you believe that something as simple as a little cleanliness helps fight depression? That's a point worth noting since, according to the National Institute of Mental Health, more than twelve million American women struggle with clinical depression each year.[2] Want a way to battle the blues that doesn't require a prescription? Simply shower, shampoo, and shine every morning! Sure, it takes effort, commitment, and discipline; but the rewards are well worth it. Good feelings follow action, not the reverse.

Personally, if I haven't showered, dressed, and groomed before breakfast, I feel *blah*. As a result, my messy appearance often expands into the other exteriors of my life—my house becomes a mess, my car gets cluttered, my laundry piles up. When these symptoms appear, I feel grimy and off-balance. A sloppy exterior is usually my first indication that my interior needs a little attention.

Light up Your Life

The second key to beauty—the kind of beauty that will attract a man worth keeping—takes no preparation, and it can be done at any time of day or night. Simply put, it's to smile—not a smirk or a halfhearted grin but a fully engaged, eye-brightening, cheek-raising, lip-curving, teeth-exposing smile. When it comes to appearance, a sincere, uninhibited smile truly makes a person. No matter your size, shape, or features, when you genuinely smile, you literally light up a room.

What if you weren't blessed with a nice smile? What if you have crooked, stained, or missing teeth—what then? Thankfully, we live in a wonderful age of convenience and privilege. Inexpensive fixes exist for almost any smile dilemma.

If your teeth are stained, for example, try an over-the-counter whitening toothpaste. For even better results, invest a little money and get mouthpieces and whitening gel from your dentist. If you have a broken tooth, check into bonding. It's an inexpensive way to make your smile look almost perfect. If your teeth need straightening, get braces. The braces used by orthodontists nowadays are far less noticeable and less cumbersome than the braces of ten or twenty years ago.

Your smile is the warmest, friendliest part of your physical appearance that you have to offer others. When you smile, you are telling people you are interested in them. Talk about the power of nonverbal communication! Doesn't your own heart warm when someone smiles at *you*? People are naturally drawn to a smiling face. Even if you don't feel happy at the moment, smile anyway. You'll feel better! A smile is the quickest and cheapest pick-me-up available. So give the gift of your most genuine smile every day. You and the people around you will be blessed. As Proverbs 15:30 says, "A cheerful look brings joy to the heart."

Besides, it's hard to be angry and bitter when you have a smile on your face. I know. My husband deliberately tries to get me to smile or laugh whenever I'm irritated at him. And it works! I can't smile and be angry at the same time.

shoulders back, chin up

"Shoulders back, stomach in, chin up—come on now, you're slouching." My mom used to say those words so often, I could almost hear them in my sleep. Yet to this day, I still have to remind myself to stand up straight! Why all the fuss? Because good posture is the third key to beauty that will attract a man worth keeping.

Much to the chagrin of feminists, chivalry is not dead, nor is being a lady. And good posture is one element of beauty that shouts to the world, "A lady has entered the courtyard." Nothing adds elegance and grace to a woman's appearance more than her stance. And yet this is the one element of beauty that most gals need to improve.

Good posture doesn't come naturally to most of us, but it's worth the effort. If you have poor posture, try the old trick of walking around the house while balancing a book on your head. If you're feeling adventurous, enroll in a ballet class, where proper posture is emphasized. Good posture will make you appear taller and more confident, improve your circulation, strengthen your back, and even firm your stomach! Not a bad payoff for pleasing your mother, wouldn't you say?

Good posture especially shines when you walk. When I was single, my girlfriends and I were determined to learn the classy walk many movie stars and models use to capture the attention of the world. The walk was fun to learn. To this day we have a code we use when one of us catches the other slouching. We whisper, "We're walking! We're walking!" Those words trigger an immediate response of beautiful posture: shoulders back, stomach in, chest out, and the front hipbones doing their stuff. By "their stuff," I mean an elegant, modified runway-model walk—*not* an exaggerated, "I'll take a hamburger with that shake" hip swing.

At first it may feel awkward to walk this way; but once you get the hang of it, you'll feel more ladylike, and the guys around you will love it. Ask your guy friends; they'll tell you. Hands down, men prefer a lady with good posture to one who slouches when she walks.

YOUR PERSONAL STYLE DEFINES YOU

Cleanliness, smiling, and good posture are the basic elements for showing off your beauty to the world of available men, but your personal style is where your personality shines through! People pick up information about your personal style through your mannerisms, idiosyncrasies, character traits, and disposition. But they also make assumptions about you based on your choice of hairstyle and clothing. Your personal style in these areas is what defines and separates you from every other woman.

You've Got the Look I've Got to Know Better

Remember the Yale University study we mentioned earlier in this chapter? According to the research, the impression you make in the first three seconds of meeting someone is based not only on your face but also on your hairstyle. In fact, your hairstyle can overpower the impact of any of your facial features—for better or for worse.[3] Who would have thought?

Dr. Marianne LaFrance, director of the Yale study, claims that your choice of hairstyle can project an image of intelligence and self-assurance or one of insecurity and conceit. For example,

LaFrance found that women wearing short, tousled hair (think Meg Ryan or Charlize Theron) are considered more confident and outgoing. Ladies with long, straight hairstyles (think Nicole Kidman or Gwyneth Paltrow) are perceived as the sexiest and most affluent. Gals with casual, medium-length hairstyles (think Liv Tyler or Sandra Bullock) are viewed as more intelligent and good-natured.

"If celebrities can change their hairstyles to play a part or make a statement, why can't you?" LaFrance says.[4] So go ahead, take control. Make your hairstyle work for you. Change your cut or color as often as you like; there's no physical pain involved. And if you don't like something, fear not! In just a few months, your hair will grow out, and you can start over. Just don't get in a rut. Update your hairstyle every once in a while to keep yourself interesting. The change doesn't have to be dramatic. But if your hair is down to your waist or your style hasn't changed in three years, you need to find a new hairdresser with some fresh ideas.

I understand how hard it is to do something different with your hair. From my teens to my early twenties, I had the same permed look. It never changed. I was definitely in a rut! Then I mustered up the courage to go in to a salon for a makeover. And you know what? As comfortable as I had been with my previous style, I grew to really like the change. I went from an outdated layered cut to a long, straight 'do. I actually began getting compliments on my hair. That was a new one for me! I really liked the attention, so the extra time it took in the morning to blow-dry my new style was worth the effort.

Since then I have changed my hairstyle a number of times. It's been shorter, longer, curly, straight, layered, flipped up, flipped down. In fact, at various times during the past ten years, I think I've expressed the whole gamut of personal styles identified in the Yale study!

The Fashion of Love

No part of your outward appearance gives off more information about your personal style than the material on your back. The fashion statement you make every time you dress tells the world what you think about yourself. Are you sloppy, sophisticated, conservative, wild, sleazy, tomboyish, snobbish, athletic, angelic, intelligent, casual, or all business? You may not be aware of it, but your clothing at any point in time gives off one of those messages.

Next time you're at the mall trying on the clothes copied from the hottest fashion magazine, try to get past the "everyone's wearing it" mentality and ask yourself, "What kind of man will this outfit attract?" Single men spend time with four types of women—female relatives, platonic friends, temporary lovers, and women worth marrying. Most men know exactly which category a woman falls into by her choice of clothing. Unfortunately, you may not realize the message your clothes are giving or how a certain guy has categorized you. That's one of the reasons many quality women lose at the game of love.

You want a husband worth keeping, not a boyfriend worth losing. So why spend your energy trying to correct a bad first impression? Make the right impression to begin with! There are two fashion extremes to avoid: the overtly provocative look that screams "temporary lover" and the tomboy look that shouts "platonic friend." Neither of these extremes will rush you down the aisle of wedded bliss.

The provocative look (overly tight T-shirts, blouses with V necks plunging down to your navel, very low-cut pants, thigh-high miniskirts worn with four-inch heels) leaves little or nothing to the imagination. When you are tempted to dress like that, ask yourself honestly, "What's my motive?" There's nothing wrong with wanting attention. Don't we all! But which response do you want to provoke in a man: "I want to sleep with that woman" or, "Wow, I want to spend time with that lady"? Men are extremely visual. That's the way God made them. So if your fashion preference says "loose woman," men will look at you and think sex, not wedding gowns and baby bonnets!

The tomboy look (sloppy or baggy jeans, oversized T-shirts and grungy tennis shoes, or other casual outfits that could be interchanged between you and your guy friends) presents a whole different set of expectations. Men may love to hang out with you, but rarely will they pursue you for romance. Even though you may be the greatest person in the world on the inside, your choice of clothing says "platonic." Few men can get past that kind of first impression.

Deciding what to wear between these two extremes depends upon the personality you want to project for the day. On a first date, for example, you may want to choose something classy and tasteful. Dress pants or a skirt and blouse would be nice. Whatever you choose, definitely dress for comfort, since anxiety is often high on a first meeting.

I have to be honest. When I was single and shopping for a new outfit for some big event—whether it was a Hollywood movie premiere or a first date—I often went for the "wow factor." I wanted to be noticed by a movie star or handsome guy. But there is a difference between standing out and going for shock value. Obviously men do pursue girls who dress for shock value (think Christina Aguilera, Jennifer Lopez, or Britney Spears), but they are seldom the women they marry. Rather, they're the ones who are pursued, conquered, and dumped. Sad. Harsh. But oh, so true.

I'm not saying that everything you wear has to be appropriate for church. Nor am I saying you can never wear extra-large T-shirts with baggy jeans or short skirts with trendy blouses. My own favorite clothes are jeans and a tank top. Just consider the circumstances and the impression you want to make, especially when you're meeting someone new.

The first time I met my husband, I was wearing an elegant, short evening dress. I'm glad I made my first impression when I was dressed my best. The second time I met him, nine months later, I was wearing sweats and a baseball cap, my hair was pulled back in a ponytail, and I had on little to no makeup. He was joining my friends and me on our Saturday hike in the hills near the famous Hollywood sign. Trust me, when I dressed that morning, I certainly didn't think I was about to meet my husband. Thankfully, we had so much fun together that we saw each other again that night for a concert. Needless to say, I cleaned myself up for the evening event.

So use discretion when you get dressed, asking yourself what message you want a man to get when he gazes upon you. Since you don't know when Mr. Right will appear, always dress neatly, in a manner appropriate for your day's activities. By dressing the way you want to be perceived, you can save yourself unnecessary heartache.

WHAT'S THE RIGHT SIZE?

What size do men want women to be? Some men prefer petite women; others prefer plus-size women. The real question is, what do *you* want for your body? Men's opinions are *not* the problem when it comes to a gal's dress size; it is we women who are obsessed. In fact, a majority of women struggle with body image, food, and weight problems. According to one American study, approximately 80 to 90 percent of women dislike their bodies. Another report shows that close to 70 percent of women are weight-preoccupied, and almost 40 percent are continually gaining and losing weight.[5]

The average woman in America is size 12, not the size 2 you see in fashion magazines. So don't be fooled into thinking that ultra-skinny fashion models are "normal." Take pride in your appearance, no matter your dress size. You can be slightly or even significantly overweight and still be clean, fashionable, and beautiful. There are many size 18 women who are happily married with children. There are also many size 2 model-types who are yearning for a husband.

The weight at which you are consistently healthy and energetic is the weight you should strive to achieve and maintain. It's at the extremes—from too large to too thin—where the health dangers lie. When I was a size 2 during my midtwenties to early thirties, I was frequently sick with throat infections, headaches, colds, and the flu, brought on by a depleted immune system and work-related stress. I'm five foot six, and I weighed between 107 and 112 pounds during those sickly years. Now I am much healthier at 120 to 125 pounds.

No one will ever be perfect. We all have at least one figure flaw.

Some imperfections are just more conspicuous than others. Believe it or not, even movie stars, singers, and models have some body part they hate! Accept yourself for who you are. Improve what is in your power to improve and learn to love or camouflage the rest.

Fire Up Your Metabolism

There are those of us with fast metabolisms and those of us with slow ones. It's not fair, but that's the way it is. Metabolism is a weird thing. We all know some skinny gal who can regularly eat Big Macs and french fries without seeming to gain an ounce. Then there are the rest of us who simply *look* at those fries and the weight piles on. Get over it! Being jealous about someone else's effortlessly trim body does nothing good for your own waistline. If you're one of those women with a slow metabolism, find the inner strength and motivation to stick with a plan to control your weight. Nothing is impossible unless you give up!

Of the seven deadly sins, my personal weakness is an inclination toward gluttony. Why do I have a constant urge to overeat? I'm probably like many of you. I overeat whenever I'm hormonal, stressed, or simply in need of a little comfort. During the past twenty years I've tried almost every fad diet on the market. And up until I had babies, I was always able to conquer my eating demons.

The minute I got pregnant, however, I gave myself license to fi-nally enjoy food. I had two glorious back-to-back pregnancies filled with plenty of divine, greasy, fattening food! But I paid a price: Nearly fifty extra pounds set up camp on my body and fought to stay there for good. It took me well over a year to lose those pesky forty-seven pounds. It also took an unwavering commitment to being trim again, major support from my girlfriends, and celebrations for each little victory. And I succeeded!

Because we all have different metabolisms and body shapes, not all diets work the same for each of us. If your goal is to lose weight, study up on the various doctor-approved weight-loss programs and chose the one to which you can remain faithful. (If you live for bread and pasta, for example, don't go on a low-carbohydrate diet!) Set goals, recruit a friend for support and accountability, write down everything you eat, and celebrate every victory, whether it's losing one pound or pulling your belt one notch tighter. If you break your diet, forgive yourself and get back to it. Never give up!

What worked best for me was a merger between two plans: Weight Watchers and Body-for-LIFE. I ate three meals a day with two small snacks to keep me from feeling hungry. In addition to eating a balance of protein and carbohydrates, I made sure my daily diet included at least two cups of steamed, boiled, grilled, or fresh vegetables; one whole apple; and eight glasses of water. I had to give up my passion for fried foods and fast-food burgers. But I did allow myself one cheat day each week (which even included an occasional chicken fried steak!).

Get Your Body Movin'

Along with my eating changes, I also began walking eight miles a week and doing weight training two days a week. I discovered that nothing in this world improves your energy or mood better than getting your blood flowing through exercise. Oh no, not the E word!

Yes, if you want to be a happy, healthy, energetic woman—and a true prize worth winning—you need to start exercising!

If you feel lethargic or moody, suffer from chronic headaches, or get winded easily, making the effort to move your body a little more each day will greatly improve your health, not to mention speed up your metabolism. You can work out intensely four or five days a week, or you can simply walk three days a week. Your body will love you either way. (Of course, you should always consult your physician before you start any workout program.)

I had such a stressful career as an agent that I was plagued with chronic tension headaches. But the cure for my head pain wasn't found in a pill. I got better simply by moving my body at least thirty minutes a day, five days a week. Sometimes I literally had to drag myself out of bed early each morning to walk up and down the hills near my home, but it worked. Not only did walking reduce my headaches, it also cleared my mind and inspired my morning devotions, since I listened to inspirational tapes while I walked.

As with dieting, I have only been able to stay faithful to a workout program by maintaining strong personal motivation. During my Hollywood days, the motivator was getting rid of my headaches; in my marriage it's to maintain my shape and have plenty of energy for my husband and family. Some people love to exercise. I've always hated it. Even though I do it consistently now, I'm not in love with the process—just the results. And since I'm always looking for the easy way out, I scour health and fitness magazines, books, and Web sites each month to keep up on nutrition and exercise trends. Here are five of my favorite monthly reads:

- *Body for Life: Twelve Weeks to Mental and Physical Strength* by Bill Phillips and Michael D'Orso, and the Body-for-LIFE Web site (www.bodyforlife.com)

- *Fitness* magazine (www.fitnessmagazine.com)

- *Prevention* magazine (www.prevention.com)

- *Shape* magazine (www.shapemagazine.com)

- *Weight Watchers* magazine (www.weightwatchers.com)

The inspiring pages in these books, magazines, and Web sites are filled with new recipes, fitness techniques, health discoveries, and much more. I highly recommend them!

THE THINGS WE DO FOR LOVE

In my never-ending attempt to pursue attractiveness, news of the latest in beauty technology always seems to catch my eye. One of the latest cosmetic crazes to sweep the country is permanent makeup.

Permanent makeup is available for lip coloring, eye lining, eyebrow tinting, and much more. A friend told me recently that her sister-in-law, Angie, was one of the first women in the country to have both lip liner and color permanently tattooed in place. A few years later, Angie suffered a skull fracture. Her family hovered over her bed in the intensive care unit, waiting for her to awaken from her coma. When Angie's eyes finally fluttered open, she didn't recognize her family at first. But she sure looked fabulous! The family got a good laugh at the irony of the situation. While Angie had a long physical recovery ahead, she didn't have to worry about look-ing bad while she was the center of attention!

I love the idea of not having to apply lipstick ever again. That option was effectively vetoed for me, however, when my husband said he thought having one permanent lip color for the rest of my life was a little too . . . well . . . permanent. But permanent eyebrows— that was another story. I am fair skinned and very blonde, and all my life I had practically invisible eyebrows. Every day I used an eyebrow pencil to darken them enough to get them to show up. Not that in-visible eyebrows are such a crisis; but I have to admit, the lure of having permanently visible brows with no daily effort on my part was appealing.

Since my husband didn't object, I made an appointment with a beauty technician called a "micropigmentologist." She actually tattooed the eyebrow color into my skin along my brow line. Since the process can be slightly painful, I opted to have my brow line numbed. What the gal didn't tell me prior to the procedure, however, was that I was going to have bright red, bloody eyebrows that would have to be covered in Vaseline for the next twenty-four hours.

That wouldn't have been a problem if I had known ahead of time and could have planned better. But that night my husband and I had a benefit to attend with the University of Oklahoma football team and legendary former football coach Barry Switzer. I may have had a Vaseline-covered forehead, but I was not about to miss the benefit! So there I was, with shiny, bright red eyebrows, boldly shak-ing hands with a room full of football players. I'm sure many things went through their minds as they looked at me, but none of them said a word. At least my husband was thoroughly entertained as he watched me through the course of the evening!

I'm ready for my closeup

When cleanliness, smiling, good posture, healthy eating, exercise, and even permanent makeup are not enough to give you the self-confidence you want to find a man worth keeping, what do you do? Do you dare venture into the world of face-altering cosmetic surgery? Wow—delicate subject! And most likely the one subject in the whole book that will generate the most mail. But I think it's important enough for me to discuss it with you as honestly as I can.

Cosmetic plastic surgery is any voluntary medical procedure done to enhance a person's outward appearance—be it a nip, a tuck, or a lift. Some are major surgeries. Others are more minor, nicknamed "lunchtime" procedures and performed in a doctor's office. Plastic surgery has become so commonplace these days that more than eight million procedures are now done in America each year (82 percent performed on females). According to the American Society of Plastic Surgery, the five most popular cosmetic procedures are nose reshaping, liposuction, breast augmentation, eyelid surgery, and facelifting. The top five nonsurgical cosmetic procedures are Botox injections, laser hair removal, microdermabrasion, chemical peels, and collagen injections.[6]

This seeming obsession with plastic surgery is reflected on the hit reality television series *Extreme Makeover*. Seven thousand people applied for the coveted, once-in-a-lifetime chance to be "made over" in the inaugural 2003 season. Only a handful were chosen, however. The sixteen winners—all deeply unhappy with various aspects of their appearance and desperate for change—were given tens of thousands of dollars' worth of cosmetic surgeries for free, performed by world-renowned cosmetic surgeons and dentists. Millions of viewers tuned in to see two people per episode come out of their shells, their personalities literally transformed by six weeks of painful but greatly desired face and body reconstruction.

I understand that opinions vary dramatically and passionately on the subject of cosmetic surgery. My stance is that it's a personal choice. If you are extremely self-conscious about a certain area of your body to the point that your daily activities and social interactions are inhibited, I think it's OK to investigate cosmetic surgery options. You may disagree with me, and that's OK. The Bible is not black, white, or even gray on the issue of surgically changing your appearance; the option simply wasn't available two thousand years ago.

Still, there are important factors to keep in mind. First of all, as we noted, many cosmetic procedures are major surgeries and therefore shouldn't be considered lightly. Since they involve risk and have results that are permanent, they probably shouldn't be your first choice for changing your appearance. Take the time to really investigate and evaluate your options for achieving your desired result short of surgery. For example, if you have a weight or shape issue, can you get the same result—albeit with more time and effort on your part—by changing your eating and exercise habits?

Understand, many people have false expectations about cosmetic surgery. If you think a medical procedure can make everything that's wrong in your life right, you'll be severely disappointed. People pursue plastic surgery to correct perceived birth defects, reconstruct body parts after an injury or burn, or otherwise make some aspect of their appearance more attractive (based on someone's subjective standard of attractiveness). In most cases, it all boils down to self-esteem. That's why the most important thing for you to evaluate if you are considering any permanent cosmetic procedure is your reason for wanting it. Though a face-lift, tummy tuck, or other procedure may improve your appearance and the first impression you give to the world, it is *not* a solution for all your self-esteem issues.

If you're considering cosmetic surgery, open your journal, write down any procedure you have in mind, and begin to thoroughly think it through. Do some initial research on the Internet. Two good Web sites to visit are www.plasticsurgery.org (The American Society of Plastic Surgeons) and www.surgery.org (The American Society for Aesthetic Plastic Surgery). After you've gained a bit of knowledge on the procedure that interests you, answer the following questions:

1. What are the pros and cons of having this procedure done? What are the risks? Do they outweigh the benefits?

2. Why do you want it done?

3. What do you hope this procedure will do for your life?

4. If that expectation is not met, how will you feel and what will you do?

A word of warning: for some people, cosmetic surgery is addictive. If you find yourself pursuing more and more facial adjustments and body surgeries, striving for some elusive concept of "perfection," you need to recognize that something much deeper is going on inside you that needs to be explored. Use the resources we mentioned in the last secret for getting help and healing.

TIPS FOR CHOOSING THE RIGHT PLASTIC SURGEON

- Get recommendations from your family doctor and from friends.

- Ask for referrals through the American Society of Plastic Surgeons (www.plasticsurgery.org) and the American Society for Aesthetic Plastic Surgery (www.surgery.org).

- Interview several doctors and check each doctor's credentials.

- Ask the doctors for a few references from previous patients and follow up on them.

- Get a price quote that includes all fees and check into payment options.

True confessions

Shortly after my Sudden Tan crisis, and long before the permanent eyebrows, I indulged in some cosmetic self-improvement myself. When I was twelve years old, I was chased by a bully at a Little League field and ran face first into the concrete Snack Shack. The result: a concussion and a broken nose.

From that moment on, I was obsessed with my profile. I just hated it. When I looked in the mirror, all I could see was that awful bump on my nose. I was convinced that every time I walked into a room, people focused on the center of my face. The only other nose like that among my family members was on the nickel in their pockets.

As I look back now at my old school pictures, I can see that my nose wasn't really that bad. But my self-esteem was decimated, and I desperately wanted a new nose. So I began to save money for rhinoplasty. I was eighteen and still living at home when I decided to have the surgery. Dad thought the idea was silly. "Why change what God gave you?" he asked. My response was that I didn't want to go through life with a bump on my nose that didn't even appear there until I was twelve years old, when that bully chased me into the Snack Shack! Thankfully, Mom was on my side, and she helped convince my dad to allow me to go through with the procedure.

What were my expectations from the surgery? I expected a perfect nose—one that looked exactly like the picture of the actress's nose I had chosen from a fashion magazine. I eagerly took the magazine with me to my doctor's appointment. I was convinced that changing my nose would make boys notice me—*finally*. That would certainly be worth all the pain I was about to suffer! Plus, I had a far-from-beautiful singing voice. Maybe, just maybe, the adjustment to my nasal passages would improve that too.

The result? I was very pleased with my new appearance—no more bump and no more insecurity about my profile. Did boys suddenly flock to me? No significant change there! In fact, no one even seemed to notice that something was different about me. Did my singing voice improve? Not one bit. Oh well!

Was it worth it to me to have the surgery? Absolutely. I removed a flaw that was affecting my fragile self-image. I grew in confidence and no longer obsessed about my appearance. So in my case, although all my expectations were not met, I still had a happy ending.

TO Tell or Not to Tell

Of course, some cosmetic procedures are less controversial than others. If you have conspicuous, unattractive moles on your face, neck, or arms, having them removed can dramatically improve your appearance—and virtually no one would judge you or call you vain for doing it. Other procedures, however, may raise a few more eyebrows.

I decided to tell you about my nose surgery because I felt the information was relevant and might be helpful to you. But back when I had it done, I didn't advertise it to anyone other than my immediate family.

If you decide to alter your image, you'll need to decide if you're going to tell other people about it. Understand, while the change may seem significant to you, it may not be obvious to others. (My rhinoplasty wasn't.) Think about the time an uncle or a guy friend shaved off his beard or mustache. You probably noticed something had changed, but you just couldn't put your finger on it. Believe it or not, the most common response when men remove facial hair or women have face-lifts or nose jobs is, "You've lost weight, haven't you?"

Cosmetic surgery is a private, personal choice. If you want people to know about your self-improvement, fine. If not, you're under no obligation to advertise it.

striving for perfection

As we close this secret, I want to add an important last word about striving for perfection in your outward appearance: *beauty doesn't guarantee happiness or even success in a relationship.* You want someone to fall in love with *you*—the person inside—not an outer shell. What's on the outside is just a pleasant bonus.

Believe it or not, beautiful women have as difficult a time finding Mr. Wonderful as the rest of us do. I have dozens of gorgeous girlfriends desperately seeking men worth keeping. And the large number of men pursuing them for the wrong reasons frustrates these gals. There are con men out there just trying to get pretty girls in bed. There are shallow men just trying to gain a trophy girlfriend to impress others. These types aren't interested in getting to know a girl's inner being. So don't think that you have to become a Barbie doll in order to have a happily-ever-after, fairy-tale life. A man worth keeping is one who is able to see beyond your outer appearance to the real you.

Please hear me on this: you are a unique and extraordinary individual. God created you to be like no one else in the entire world. You are special, and you deserve a man who is special. So start treating yourself that way!

Yes, commit yourself to taking steps to improve the first impression you make on others. But relax! No one attains a perfect appearance. Perfection is an elusive fantasy. Simply apply the basics of beauty we've discussed in this secret, then proudly accept yourself for who you are. I promise, the rest of the world will respond.

LET THE WORLD KNOW You're Free

Sitting on the bright leather couch on the fourth floor in my Beverly Hills office, my producer client took a moment's break from discussing his upcoming movie.

"You're still single, Victorya?" Neil asked. "I just don't get it. If I were single . . ."

"I'm still single, but I've always got my eyes open," I told him.

"I know a lot of single guys. What are you looking for?"

"Someone with the four Ss—single, sexy, successful, and saved. You find me someone like that, and I'd be thrilled." (At that point I hadn't added my fifth S: sane.)

"I get the first three. But 'saved'?" Neil asked with a raised eye-brow. "Come on, we're in Hollywood, honey. How about settling for 'chosen' [Jewish]? Single, sexy, successful, and chosen—it has a nice ring to it. Three out of four ain't bad!"

"Now, Neil, you know how obsessed I am about my faith," I said. "Any man dating me would be bored to tears if he didn't share my beliefs."

"Hmm. I guess I'll just have to find out who's saved around here."

OK, you've dedicated the time to finding out what you want in a man. You've identified your ideal future, and you've started making the necessary changes to your present to help get you there. You're *really* ready to find your man worth keeping. So what's next? Do you shout, "Hello? Here I am! I'm a great catch! Where's my man?"

All too often I hear women drone on and on about how there are "no good men out there." Yet few of them are willing to ask others to help them look. Yoo-hoo! Why not? Why try to do it all on your own? Finding a man worth keeping—someone you'll commit the rest of your life to, someone with whom you'll probably make babies and begin a whole new generation—is far too crucial a process to go through in a vacuum. It's time to let the world know you're free!

Does the thought of asking for help with dating make you want to hyperventilate? Don't write off the idea yet. Just be open to the possibility that you *may* go public with your manhunt and keep on reading.

What I'm really talking about is enlisting cheerleaders. I mean, think about it. Jesus had his disciples, the president has a cabinet, the queen has her court, celebrities have entourages, Moses had Aaron, Joshua had Caleb, Naomi had Ruth, Mary had Martha. I could go on and on. What's my point? Everyone needs supporters.

Everyone needs a cheering section. If being single is indeed a waiting game—an important *championship* waiting game at that—then it follows that you need your own crowd to cheer you on.

I strongly believe in setups, blind dates, and good, old-fashioned matchmaking. All three require the deliberate help of people who are willing to cheer for you, who honestly want you to win in the game of love. Who in your life has your best interests at heart? You need to track down these people and draft them onto your cheering squad!

WHO'S CHEERING FOR YOU?

Pull out your journal and write each of these titles on separate pages: "Family," "Coworkers," "Old Friends/School Friends," "Church Friends," "Neighbors," and "Miscellaneous Acquaintances" (e.g., your pastor, accountant, doctor, dentist, dry cleaner, and so on). Now, under each of these categories, write the names of people you feel would have your best interests at heart. Who might enjoy setting you up? Who hangs around exciting people? Who has a unique career or ministry where interesting men may be found? Who loves to meddle in people's affairs?

Hooray! You now have a cheering squad you can invite to meddle in your life. Since the beginning of time, people have loved sticking their noses into other people's business. Give your cheerleaders your permission—and your blessing—to stick their noses into yours!

Personally, I was so obsessed with finding my husband, I had no problem letting the world know I was free. It just made sense to me. As a result, I met many intriguing men I would never have known

if someone had not deliberately introduced us. Not to mention—
hello!—I met my husband through a friend who was willing to get
involved.

HAVE I GOT SOMEONE FOR YOU!

At this very moment, there is a whole multitude of single, available,
Christian men in this world you simply don't have access to . . . yet.
Choose to be open to the possibility that a man worth keeping just
might be waiting to meet *you*. Now recruit your cheering squad to
help you find him. What are the benefits of allowing your cheerleaders to intervene? First, you'll be introduced to men who are otherwise out of reach since you have no other way of meeting them.
Second, setups are gentle on your ego. And third, the guy gets to
stay in the lead in the developing relationship. Let's take a moment
to look at each of these benefits more closely.

Meeting the unreachables

Tina works in the world of cardiologists, technicians, and nurses.
Married, outgoing, and seemingly friends with everyone, she has access to successful, available men that most single women don't. She
is a perfect matchmaker candidate. And sure enough, Tina has fun
doing exactly that—setting up introductions between her single
friends who would otherwise never have a chance to meet. She
even proudly attended the wedding of one couple she introduced!

If you are willing to allow your cheerleaders to set you up on
blind dates, the potential is there for you to be introduced to coveted unreachables, such as athletes, celebrities, doctors, pilots, and
politicians, not to mention many other great guys. By approaching

friends like Tina who have connections to eligible men, you can literally aim for the stars without becoming a stalker or pursuer. You'll never know who your friends and acquaintances know until you ask! Baseball great Mark McGwire was set up with a close family friend of mine who could pass for a clone of Brooke Shields, so you can imagine how thrilled the baseball legend was with his matchmaker!

keeping your ego intact

You can pretend you don't have an ego, but you'd be kidding yourself. We all feel vulnerable when we step out of our comfort zone to share our feelings and express an interest in a particular person. That's why it's so great to enlist the aid of friends. Having a third party suggest to a particular guy that you might be a match allows that guy to agree or disagree without coming off as presumptuous or rude. If he chooses not to move forward and ask you out, you can both pretend the rejection never happened. Hooray for saving face!

Two of the times I was able to save face, with only minor bruises to my ego, involved crushes I had on movie stars. Like millions of other women, I used to get starry-eyed when I saw George Clooney or Greg Kinnear on the big screen. Through my circle of influence as a Hollywood agent, I had ways to gain introductions to both. I knew one of George Clooney's relatives and one of Greg Kinnear's best friends. I expressed my interest to my colleagues as delicately as possible.

George has a lot of Christian relatives, so I figured the odds were good that he cared about God too. However, because I had made my husband wish list known, George's relative chose not to make the introduction. (I was looking for marriage; the actor was not.)

Moving on to my next rejection, actor Greg Kinnear's buddy made introductions for us on several occasions. Greg knew about my crush. Although he was always nice to me, he never took the leap to ask me out. My ruffled ego was soothed when I discovered later that he met his wife at about the same time he was introduced to me.

Letting the Guy Lead

My friend Mike couldn't believe it. It was summer, and he had been working long, thirteen-hour days on a pressing deadline. Coming home exhausted one evening, he was shocked to see Cindy—a girl he'd met only once before through a friend, and who lived in another state—standing in the middle of his driveway.

"Surprise!" Cindy gushed before informing Mike she was planning to stay in town for a few days.

Is this some kind of fatal attraction? Mike wondered. He'd enjoyed talking with Cindy when they first met, and he had hoped to see her again. But for her to show up out of the blue was not only poor timing, it felt to Mike as if she were forcing something prematurely. The warm feelings he'd had for Cindy after their first meeting evaporated like dew in the morning sun.

I'm convinced a man should always be the pursuer. I know this flies in the face of political correctness, but God designed men to lead and women to follow. Ladies, it is perfectly fine to guide, direct, and suggest, but the man needs to always *think* he is leading, especially at the beginning of a relationship. God created man to be the aggressor, and a man's instinct is to conquer. Two great benefits of allowing your friends to intervene in your love life are that this plays to a man's nature, and you never have to be the one in pursuit.

If you have an interest in someone, ask a mutual friend to put the word out. The guy can then choose to ask you out or not. Thus, you are only indirectly pursuing him—a technicality that doesn't count in my book. The man remains in the driver's seat and decides whether to make a move. He has nothing to fear if he's interested in you, because he already knows you're interested too. Whatever you do, just don't show up on his doorstep and shout, "Surprise!"

HOW TO ASK FOR HELP

Let's say you've mustered up enough courage to let the world know you're free. Now what? Go back through your journal. Remember the slogan or catch phrase you came up with in secret 1? (If you were stumped, I offered you the free use of my five Ss—single, sexy, successful, saved, and sane.) Revisit that page and rehearse your wishlist slogan. Now prepare to present it to your cheering section.

The next time you see any of your cheerleaders (if the timing is right, of course), give them permission to meddle in your life. Say something like, "Finding a cute, available Christian guy sure is tough sometimes. Have you seen one lately?" Or, "Hey, where does a good Christian girl go to find a great guy? I sure could use some help." Hopefully, they'll respond like my friend Neil did and ask, "What exactly are you looking for?"

Keep It Light

When you first start letting the world know you're single and free, be light and nonchalant. Always make it easy for your friend, family member, or acquaintance to decline to help you find a man without feeling guilty. It's no one's obligation to help you, of course; so if your request makes someone uncomfortable, hold no grudge. This process should be fun for everyone—you, your potential date, and your matchmaker.

Besides, your long-term relationships with the people in your life are more important than a one-time shot at romance. Let's say a girlfriend decides to stay out of your love life. You know she cares for you. So what's up? Her decision is probably in your best interest. Maybe she knows she's not a good judge of character. Maybe she's shy. Or maybe she's an incessant people pleaser who's terrified of playing a role in a game where someone could get hurt. So if you're rebuffed, let it slide. Then move on to someone else on your cheering squad. I promise, if you keep asking, *someone* in your life will want to help.

The Real World

The adrenaline rush of hope and anticipation is what keeps you in the dating game, right? With each new date, perspiration beads on your upper lip as you wait in fear of disappointment or rejection, while clinging to a glimmer of hope that this time, things will be different. This just might be *him*. I know every heart-pounding part of the game. When I say I've been on a lot of blind dates, I mean a *lot*—I would hazard to guess a hundred. Believe me, reaching that number took a lot of cheerleaders and matchmakers! And here's the hard reality: all but one of those relationships ultimately ended in disappointment.

Welcome to the world of personal taste! There's no guarantee that you'll like the person you meet, no matter how adamantly your cheerleaders insist, "Oh, but the two of you are perfect for each other!" Their assessment may be due to something I call "friendship goggles"—the blurry vision friends sometimes possess when it comes to seeing another friend's attractiveness or compatibility. There's no guarantee your date will even remotely match the description you've been given by your "reliable" sources. I was shocked many times at the contrast between the descriptions friends gave and the actual men who showed up on my doorstep!

To enjoy the game of matchmaking, then, you need to adopt the attitude that you will just go with the flow. Approach every blind date with the thought, *I'm meeting someone new today, and maybe— just maybe—he'll be the one.*

One word of advice: if you're only willing to date extremely attractive men, be very direct about that fact with your friends. But trust me on this one: looks aren't everything. A lot of gorgeous guys rang my doorbell, but you couldn't *pay* me to dine with some of them a second time. Looks may be skin-deep, but shallow is clear to the bone.

WHEN CHEERLEADERS COME UP SHORT

What if all your cheerleaders come up empty-handed? In today's world of dating, there is more than one way to meet your potential mate. Of course, you should approach any potential relationship cautiously; but if you decide to explore matchmaking options outside your circle of friends and relatives, I encourage you to keep your "man worth keeping" antenna finely tuned. At least when you're set up by a friend, you have that friend vouching for your date. That's not the case when you use other options, which may include:

- Singles groups at local churches

- Clubs focusing on a favorite hobby or activity

- Dating services

- Becoming your own matchmaker

Let's take a closer look at each of these options.

Exploring Singles Groups at Local Churches

I'll be honest. When I first moved to Los Angeles, I specifically searched for a church with an active singles group. That was one of the more important factors for me in looking for a home church. I desperately wanted to meet new female friends and—cutting to the chase—available Christian men.

I often hear Christians say that choosing a church based on available men is wrong. "Church is a place to seek God with no other agenda," I've been told. Obviously the most important reason to find a church home is to have a place to worship Jesus and get sound Bible teaching. But if you eliminate church as an option for meeting potential dates, where do you turn? The workplace? A bar? I hope not.

The first few weeks in a new church can be intimidating. When I was "the visitor," I forced myself to walk up and introduce myself to at least three people—male or female—every Sunday. I also bravely attended any socials or events that sounded intriguing, even if I went alone and knew no one. (Yes, I'm patting myself on the back. If you drum up the courage to take these steps, you should pat yourself on the back too.)

You may argue that it's the church's responsibility to reach out to new folks. That may be true, but when you're new to a community and desperate to get connected, take my lead. Don't let months slip by needlessly. Be bold, stick out your hand, and make the first move. Who knows? If you happen to meet someone else who is new, you just may have found a lifelong friend!

HOW TO GET THE MOST OUT OF CHRISTIAN SINGLES ACTIVITIES

- Visit various singles groups, Sunday school classes, and weeknight church meetings.
- Shake hands and introduce yourself to at least three new people per meeting.
- Grab a girlfriend and attend social events listed in the church bulletin or calendar.
- If you can't find a friend to go with you, be brave and go alone.
- Vacation at singles retreats sponsored by your denomination.

joining the club

Another great way to let the world know you're free is to join a group or club that's centered on one of your favorite hobbies or activities. What do you like to do outside of work that could provide an opportunity for meeting available men? Are you into hiking, biking, climbing, swimming, cars, motorcycles, missions, politics, fund-raisers, or charities? There's an organization for almost every interest!

Open your journal and make a page titled "Hobbies." Write down everything you can think of that would be fun for you to do outside of work. Then commit to finding a group or club that is involved in one of those things and go have a good time! You're likely to meet some fun people in the process. And maybe, just maybe, one of them will turn out to be a man worth keeping.

checking out Dating services

At the encouragement of her girlfriend, thirty-seven-year-old Suzanne logged onto an Internet dating service for a lark, not really expecting anything to come of it. Soon, however, she began exchanging e-mails with a man named David, thirty-eight; and about a month later, the two decided to meet. David was an avid soccer player, coach, and fan, so they agreed to attend a soccer game of the daughter of Suzanne's friend—a safe, public environment for a first meeting. They hit it off, and David even met the approval of Suzanne's friend and her husband. Within a year they were engaged; and later, they were married.

Suzanne still can't believe she was able to find a fabulous *Christian* man on the Internet. "Ironically, David was the first Christian man I ever dated," she says. "That was a huge bonus and something I wouldn't change for the world."

The traditional dating services of the 1980s and '90s are fast being replaced by new Internet dating services like the one Suzanne used. A handful of matchmaking organizations and in-person dating services still exist, such as Great Expectations, a national dating service that has been around since the 1970s. These companies still provide face-to-face, personalized assistance in their offices. But the number of online dating services has literally exploded.

DATING SERVICE TIPS

If you decide to try out a dating service, follow these tips:

- Don't reveal your personal information (last name, address, phone number) until you are sure the guy is safe. Most anyone can track you down on the Internet if they know your last name and the state in which you reside.

- If a guy pushes for a face-to-face meeting before you're comfortable with the idea, listen to the alarm bells that should be ringing in your head. A man worth keeping will wait until you are ready.

- Don't initiate. Let the guy take the lead in moving forward, whether that involves continued e-mails, a phone call, or an in-person meeting.

- Set up a separate e-mail address just for online dating. Again, don't reveal your last name or other traceable personal information. Yahoo and Hotmail are two e-mail services that keep your personal information private.

- Whether you use a personal or online dating service, choose your photo wisely. Risqué or sexy photographs will give the wrong impression and attract the wrong kind of guy—even on a Christian dating site.

- Strongly consider doing a background check on an interesting man before accepting a date.

- Find more common-sense tips and advice on how to navigate a Christian dating site by checking out www.ChristianDatingService.com.[1]

The upside of dating services is that your potential suitors are serious about finding a relationship; otherwise, they wouldn't spend the money it costs to participate. Plus, you get to read about the guys and see photos of them before you agree to date them. Sometimes even videos are available. The downside is that many services are expensive (although some do offer free trial periods). Also, if you're the sensitive type, you may feel a little embarrassed about admitting that you've resorted to a dating service. But whatever the past stigma was that has been attached to dating services, it is fast dissipating. Nowadays they're much more accepted as a viable option for meeting new people.

If you feel adventurous, here are a few popular Christian dating sites to explore:

- Single Christian Network (www.singlec.com)
- Christian Cafe (www.christiancafe.com)
- Christian Singles Connection (www.singles.org)
- eharmony.com (www.eharmony.com)

Of course, many online dating sites are not exclusively Christian, like the one Shawna inadvertently happened upon. Finishing research at her desk one day, an ad flashed on her computer screen: "Are you lonely? Click here." Having ended a long-term relationship three months earlier, Shawna was intrigued, took the bait, and clicked. She was directed to the Web site www.Match.com. She was bored, so she filled out the form of goofy questions and laughed as she pressed Submit, fully expecting a request for money to pop up—at which point she fully intended to choose Decline. Instead, the screen said, "Thank you for filling out a profile. Your profile will be posted in twenty-four hours."

At first Shawna panicked. But after telling her Christian girlfriend what she had done, they both got a good laugh and decided Shawna had nothing to fear or to lose since she had made it clear in her profile she was looking for a committed Christian man. Within two weeks she got two "hits" from duds—men who obviously hadn't read her profile. Then one day, as she was scrolling through the silly e-mail names of alleged matches (ranging from LatinLover to Theoneforyou), one user name jumped out at her—BiolaUniversity.

BiolaUniversity? That was the name of a Christian school, and her alma mater! Leery of the coincidence, Shawna requested that BiolaUniversity e-mail her from the school's computer to verify he really attended there. He did. The guy's name was Dale. Not only did he work and live nearby, he really did go to Biola, and he claimed to love God as much as Shawna did. Wow!

Deciding to give him a chance, Shawna began e-mailing back and forth with Dale. Eventually she felt comfortable enough to meet him. And while it wasn't love at first sight, they clearly had a rapport. In time, they fell in love and got married. To this day Shawna is still blown away at how God delivered her man worth keeping in his perfect timing. "God used a silly pop-up ad at work and a non-Christian Web site to bring me my amazing, devout Christian husband!" she raves.

While Suzanne and Shawna and many other women have had positive experiences with dating services, I think it's wise to add a word of caution here. If you're contemplating going out with a complete stranger—even one you've been communicating with for some time by e-mail—do some investigating before committing to a date. As one *USA Today* reporter put it, "With the mere click of a mouse, you can stumble across a serial killer just as easily as your soul mate."[2]

A recent poll even claimed that one third of the alleged 6.7 million members of online dating services are in reality married.[3]

With potential danger lurking, several sites have emerged to assist you in your quest for truth and safety in dating. For a small fee, these companies will do background checks on potential dates. Typical information that can be traced includes a person's name, address, birth date, marital status, education, employment, income, bankruptcies, liens, judgments, criminal record, and sex offender status. Some of these sites include www.knowx.com, www.records.com, www.ussearch.com, and www.VerifiedPerson.com. What I like about Verified Person is that it's a self-verification service. Not only do you get to see what a trace reveals about you and your past (very interesting!), you also gain a bargaining chip to compel your potential date to go through the verification process. After all, you aren't asking him to do anything you haven't done yourself.

Another online site worth mentioning doesn't do background checks, but it does offer a helpful service. Called LookBetterOnline (www.lookbetteronline.com), it promises to create a more appealing photograph for you to use with your online dating profile. The photos aren't "glamour shots," but rather quality professional photos designed to reflect your personality. According to the site, four out of five of its customers get at least two times more responses and e-mails from potential dates when they include a new LookBetterOnline photo with their online profiles. Maybe it's worth a try!

Cheryl met her husband, not through an online dating service, but through an online chat room for her favorite hobby: computer technology. Aware that the stranger she was communicating with could be an ax murderer, Cheryl took great precautions not to reveal traceable personal information about herself. After e-mailing with the man for quite a while, she finally gave him a phone number (her parents') and set up a time for him to call when she'd be visiting them. Over time she began to feel comfortable enough to meet this man and chose a restaurant—a nice, very public place—for their first face-to-face contact.

Cheryl was pleasantly surprised when a handsome man arrived at the restaurant for lunch. Wanting to know if he was really a committed Christian, she slyly played the role of a searching nonbeliever to test whether he really knew his stuff. He did. In fact, he was quite the effective witness, even on a first date! She was impressed. And as you might guess, they eventually married. They now have three adorable children.

Suzanne, Shawna, and Cheryl took precautions to make sure their online friends weren't dangerous. For your own safety, I urge you to do the same.

Becoming Your Own Matchmaker

There is a way you can be your own matchmaker without becoming a pursuer. It's called flirting, and it's done with eye contact, smiles, and body language. For example, if you're in a room that includes one or more interesting men, standing with your arms uncrossed sends the message that you're open to meeting people. Standing with your shoulders back and stomach tight means you're confident. If you look invitingly into a man's eyes, smile, then casually turn away, you give the impression you may be interested.

Dr. Pat Allen coined the famous "five-second flirt" in her book *Getting to I Do*. When you see an interesting man, "the first thing you want to do is get into his line of sight," she writes. "When you catch his eye, you must give him the most inviting and receptive look you can manage, for three seconds. Count them. Eye contact, eye contact, eye contact. No quick counts, no matter how nervous you get." She goes on to say that if you maintain a fourth and fifth second of eye contact, you make your romantic interest clear.[4]

When I was single, I tried the five-second flirt. But to be honest, five seconds felt like an eternity. I found that three solid seconds was a comfortable length of time for me to look at a man and send the message that I had noticed him and liked what I saw. If the man was interested in me, he would invariably walk over and strike up a conversation. If he didn't, that was fine. I didn't have to feel insecure or rejected, because I hadn't said anything. All I'd done was briefly look at him and smile.

Here's an assignment for the next week. Identify at least three single men you find attractive, and practice the art of the three-second flirt (or the five-second flirt if you feel daring). Make eye contact in the hallway after church, at work, at a party, or any other place where you notice a handsome man. See what happens. The wonderful benefit of nonverbal flirting is that it gives the man a sign that it's OK to approach you. You aren't the pursuer; you're simply acknowledging by your gaze and smile that you're intrigued. I realize this assignment may cause you to step out of your comfort zone. But do it anyway, and have fun in the process!

INCREASED EXPOSURE, EXPANDED TERRITORY

All the ideas presented in this chapter will increase your exposure to potential mates. How about deciding right now to try one new option each week to expand your territory and increase your opportunities for meeting a man worth keeping? Call a cheerleader. Attend a singles group. Pursue a hobby. Check out a dating service. Or take matters into your own hands and try a little flirting. Let the world know you're free!

Are you still hesitant? Amy, one of my married girlfriends, displayed a look of horror when I mentioned I was writing a chapter on matchmaking. So I asked, "Didn't you go on blind dates before you got married?"

"No," she quickly responded.

"How did you meet your husband then?"

Amy paused for a long moment. "Well, I thought he was cute," she finally said. "I knew him in passing, but we had never really met. So I said something to a mutual friend, and she made the official introduction for us."

"So you were set up?"

"Well, yeah, I guess I was!" she admitted.

Ask the married couples you know how *they* met. I'll bet half, if not more, were introduced by a friend. So don't let anyone—including yourself—convince you there's something wrong with getting outside help. By letting the world know you're free, you're actively opening yourself up to new people and potential new relationships. That's a good thing!

Of course, you're also opening yourself up for potential heartbreak (unless you're lucky enough to meet your mate on your first try). Very likely, you'll accumulate your fair share of horror stories of geeks, creeps, and really bad evenings. But one thing's for sure: your life will never be boring!

So go ahead. Step out of your comfort zone. Collect your cheer-leaders and ask for help. If you've already asked, ask again. You say you've been disappointed? Join the club! None of us is exempt from disappointment and discouragement. But even if your last date was a dud, don't give up. I certainly had my share of flops; yet I can hap-pily tell you that in my case, the benefits of enlisting help out-weighed the risks. You'll never know what God has in store for you if you don't persevere.

In 1942 the general manager of the St. Louis Cardinals, Branch Rickey, said of baseball player Yogi Berra, "He'll never make any-thing more than a triple-A ballplayer at best." Hearing that verdict, Yogi could have given up and gone home. Instead he coined the phrase "It ain't over till it's over." With that simple truism as his motto, Yogi went on to become a fifteen-time major-league all-star. He played in fourteen World Series and holds numerous World Series records, including hitting the first pinch-hit home run in World Series history. In a player and coaching career spanning fifty years, Yogi Berra rewrote baseball history.[5]

So take a tip from Yogi. When you strike out in love, just say, "It ain't over till it's over." Then stay in the game! If you hang in there long enough, you just might find your man worth keeping.

SEEK DIVINE *Intervention*

Carolyn has spent thousands of dollars trying to become the perfect catch. She has the looks, the body, the personality, and the connections to find a great man. And yet, after a few months of dating a new guy, she typically discovers that he's just another dud. Or worse, he's a good guy, but there's no chemistry between them. Ugh! She's so frustrated!

Taking a bold step, Carolyn went to a therapist known as the "relationship guru to the stars." *Wow*, she thought, *if it works for the stars, it will surely work for me!* Five years and untold dollars later, she has learned how to flirt, volume date, even guarantee a second or third date. But still no ideal man has arrived.

Carolyn is a dear friend of mine. Yet no matter how often we chat about her dating life, I can't seem to convince her to seek divine intervention from the Ultimate Therapist. Though Carolyn asked God into her life about the same time she met her relationship guru, she relegated God to Sundays and left romance to her guru.

I'm going to speak to you from my heart of hearts now. I want you to really pay attention and grasp the secret I'm about to share. I can't force you to follow any of the ten dating secrets in this book, even though I'm sure you'll improve your chances of getting married if you follow at least one or two of them. But this book isn't about marrying just *any* man. I want you to find the very best man for you. That's why, if you really want to find a man worth keeping, I beg you to master this secret: *seek divine intervention*. Even if this is the only secret out of the ten that you follow, we both will have been successful.

That's why I have to ask, have you gone to the Creator of the world yet and sought his active involvement in your life? I'm talking about pursuing an intimate, daily relationship with the One who made you. I don't know how long you've known God. Perhaps you met him as a child, or in high school, or after college. Maybe you were introduced to him when you went with a friend to see Mel Gibson's film *The Passion of the Christ*. Maybe you just met God this week.

Or maybe you don't really know him yet. If that's your case, don't stop reading. This secret is for you too.

When I was a little girl, my concept of seeking God was making sure my "fire insurance" was up to date by immediately confessing any sin. I was terrified I'd get into an accident and die before I could repent one more time and prevent a one-way trip to hell. But you know what? Seeking God and having a relationship with him is so much more than keeping up payments on an insurance policy.

Don't get me wrong. Having a quick-to-repent heart is a plus for any Christian. But I eventually came to understand that my fire insurance was paid in full once and for all when I asked Jesus to come into my heart. I was twenty-three when I discovered Ephesians 2:8–9, a wonderful Bible passage that assures me I'm saved by God's grace and not by my own performance. You have no idea the depth of burden that was lifted from me when I realized my own perfection was not the requirement for my salvation! Jesus offered his life for me as a free gift. I merely had to accept that precious gift and ask him to intervene in my life from that day forward. Now the daily choices I make to obey him are a reflection of my love for him, not a futile attempt to earn my way to heaven. And every day is a wonderful adventure!

HOW TO KNOW GOD

Do you have an ongoing, personal relationship with God—one in which you talk to him about everything in your life and allow him to talk to you? Do you know him truly, intimately, *really*? If not, then I have to tell you, you're missing out on the greatest romance in the universe. The fact is, whether you recognize it or not, there is a void in your life that no man and no love on earth can fill. God alone can fill that empty space with his perfect, everlasting love. You will never know a greater love than the love God has for you! It's no coincidence that when you know God, *really* know him, you become part of what the Bible calls the bride of Christ.[1]

What does it mean to know God? Certainly, we can know *about* someone without knowing him or her personally. For example, we can know a lot about singer Jessica Simpson by reading magazines or watching TV. But how many of us have her cell phone number? If you have exchanged private phone numbers with Jessica and are chatting on a regular basis, I would call that knowing her personally. Active, ongoing communication is the difference between knowing someone personally and merely knowing about that person.

A lot of people tell me they "believe in God" or "know a lot about God." But neither statement is enough to change their lives.

Do you *know* him?

Let me encourage you to seek to know God personally. Read his divinely inspired, autobiographical book, the Bible. Study it daily and make it your life manual. Seek to know God by asking him to give you wisdom, favor, and joy.

Seek to know God by talking to him about every area of your daily life—including your dream for a husband. After all, God already knows everything about you. One reading of Psalm 139 makes that clear. Here is just an excerpt from verses 1 through 16:

> O LORD, you have searched me and you know me.
>
> You know when I sit and when I rise; you perceive my thoughts from afar. . . . Before a word is on my tongue you know it completely, O LORD.
>
> You hem me in—behind and before; you have laid your hand upon me. . . .
>
> For you created my inmost being; you knit me together in my mother's womb.
>
> I praise you because I am fearfully and wonderfully made. . . .
>
> All the days ordained for me were written in your book before one of them came to be.

What's my point? God created you. He knows you. He's waiting for you to seek to know him too!

AS EASY AS ABC

I'm a simple person, so I like to keep things simple. The easiest way for me to describe how you can truly know God is by turning to the ABCs.

A is for "ask." Jesus said, "Here I am! I stand at the door and knock. If anyone hears my voice and opens the door, I will come in" (Revelation 3:20). Simply ask God to come into your heart and intervene in your life. He's just waiting for the invitation!

B is for "believe." Believe Jesus is who he said he is. When Jesus was on the earth, he made a lot of profound statements, including blatantly claiming that he was God (2 John 10:30). Jesus said he was sent to the earth in the flesh to be the ultimate sacrifice for all sin. He willingly died, was buried, was raised from the dead three days later, and went to heaven to prepare a place there for us. To learn more about Jesus, who he is, and what he said, read the entire Gospel of John (the fourth book of the New Testament). And start believing!

C is for "confess." All of us have done bad or misguided things that, thank goodness, others don't know about. But God knows. Confess your sins to God and ask him to forgive you. He will, as 1 John 1:9 makes clear. He's the God of fresh starts! Ask, believe, confess—and you will begin a journey of divine intervention that will not only guarantee you eternal life but also an exciting adventure here on earth.

Jesus promises to come into your heart and begin revealing his plans for you. If you've just made the decision to know God and seek divine intervention for the first time, here is a simple prayer you can pray right now:

Dear Father, please forgive me for all that I've done wrong. I believe that Jesus died on the cross for *me*.

Please come into my heart right now and take control of my life. I just don't do well on my own! I give you every part of my life, even the delicate area involving my dream for a husband. Teach me to trust you as you prepare me for the husband you've designed just for me. In Jesus's name I pray, amen.[2]

LET GO AND LET GOD

If you've made the decision to allow God to intervene in your life, whether for the first time or the fifty-first, don't stop now. What a loss it would have been if I'd asked for God's intervention one moment and then said "that's enough" the next—no growing close to God, no delving into the Bible, no seeking his plan for my life. Yet I am amazed at how many Christians do just that. They miss out on the greatest adventure of life from Monday through Saturday because they don't pursue God beyond Sunday morning.

More to our point, I'm amazed at how many single women say they leave God out of their husband search—even ladies who have known Jesus most of their lives. These are the same women who don't think twice about calling on God for help on a final exam or an important job interview. They'll pray for peace, healing, even for a cute guy to notice them. But in the intimate details of their husband search, they demand full control—terrified that God, if consulted, will deliver an ugly bore.

Are you afraid that God's best man for you is a complete nerd? That's not the God I serve. The Bible says that God cares about every aspect of your life. He knows you in detail; He keeps track of your sorrows and collects every tear you shed. And His desire is to bless you and give you abundant life.[3] Wow! If that's true, certainly God cares about the man you choose to marry. After all, it's *the* very most important decision you'll ever make, after your choice to follow Christ. Generations to come will be affected by your decision. I would call that significant!

I'm going to ask you to do something scary. It may be contrary to everything you feel inside right now, but I'm going to ask you to take the risk and do it anyway. I want you to let go of the white-knuckled grip you have on your desperate search for your mate and let God bring you the man of your dreams. Jesus said, "Take my yoke upon you and learn from me, for I am gentle and humble in heart, and you will find rest for your souls. For my yoke is easy and my burden is light" (Matthew 11:29–30). You don't have to carry this burden alone! Besides, who else but God knows you better than you know yourself? Who else knows exactly what you need at any moment?

God says in Psalm 46:10, "Be still, and know that I am God." In modern English that means, "Chill out!" Relax and quietly contemplate God's power. Let go of your all-consuming obsession to have the husband of your dreams. Let go and trust God with your future.

"Let go? Are you crazy? If I relinquish control, I'll never find my husband," you may object. I certainly can relate to that fear. I lived it for quite some time. And I'm a certified control freak. But the payoff of letting go is huge! It wasn't until I let go of the viselike grip I had on my husband plans that I began to enjoy life. I became free to enjoy the moments of my life, and I began an exciting adventure in the midst of my singleness. *That's* what I want for you.

If your heart aches in loneliness or you feel God has forgotten you, please know that I understand your pain. I endured many similar moments. Even though I struggled with loneliness and deeply mourned the heartache of failed relationships, I made the conscious decision to trust God through good guys, bad guys, and no guys. I determined to keep on living, pursuing my career, and making grandiose plans for my future. Through the pain, I chose to seek God's intervention in my life. And not only did I survive, I thrived, emerging from the process stronger, wiser, and ultimately happier.

As a bonus, God graciously allowed me to enjoy the weddings of many friends and family members without feeling jealousy. (Really!) After all, I wanted my *own* husband, not theirs.

Did I ever regress and take back control? Yes; too often, I confess. I did some dumb things to "help" God find me a man when it seemed he was too busy or not interested. One of the ways I "helped" was by dating non-Christians. On a few occasions, I got angry and stopped speaking to God completely. But every single time I took over, I got hurt.

And God always wooed me back. In the midst of my tears, he would wrap me in his arms of comfort and peace. Then he'd whisper to my soul, *It's OK, Victorya. I'm still here. I never left you. I was just waiting for you to trust me again. I know the plans I have for you— exciting, wonderful plans. It will be worth the wait. You'll see.*[4]

If you feel God isn't interested in answering your prayers for a husband, perhaps you have been hurt or disappointed by a man in your past—a father, a boyfriend, maybe an ex-husband who deserted you. Is that hurt keeping you from pursuing a relationship with your perfect, loving heavenly Father? Is anger toward a man—or maybe toward God—keeping you from seeking divine intervention in your life? If so, I encourage you to tell God how you feel. He already knows anyway. I was so thrilled when I learned that God can handle my anger. In the same way I can handle my three-year-old's tantrum without loving her any less, God can handle my honestly expressed emotions. He can handle yours too.[5]

Trust me on this: God is not out to make your life miserable. He cares for you. He wants the best for you. He hurts when you hurt. On the cross Christ bore not only our sins, but also our pain. There is nothing we can go through that Jesus Christ did not experience physically or emotionally when he was on the earth. He was wounded and rejected by those he loved, just as many of us have been wounded and rejected. He understands!

So let go of the fear that God doesn't have the time or interest to bless you with a husband. Instead, offer him control over this delicate area of your life. Granted, allowing God to be in charge is difficult—excruciatingly so at times. But I'm confident you'll discover what I discovered: that trusting God is worth every tear you will ever shed, because it will pay off big time. I love my life! Each day I reap the rewards of my choice to let go and let God.

Proverbs 3:5–6 says, "Trust in the LORD with all your heart; do not depend on your own understanding. Seek his will in all you do, and he will direct your paths" (NLT). If you seek God's will in every area of your life, including your search for a man worth keeping, he promises to guide your steps. God will not let you down. He is already involved. Why don't you get on speaking terms so you can hear him when he says, *Look—over there. He's the one!*

CAN WE TALK?

Open your journal again and pull out the husband wish list you created in secret 1. Now find a quiet place where you can sit down and candidly talk to God about your dreams. (Do this as often as you like. God loves to hear from you! He never checks his caller ID and lets the answering machine pick up.)

Your quiet place may be a corner in your home, a park bench, a grassy spot next to a lake, or on the beach. Allow at least thirty minutes to pray over your list. Ask God to show you anything that needs to be added or removed from it.

Next, ask God to bless your list and prepare the man it describes to meet you soon. Copy and date your latest version, and place it wherever you will see it daily—for example, on your bathroom mirror or car visor, or in your Bible or day planner. As I said in secret 1, I kept mine in my day planner for more than five years, until my wedding day. Each day I read it and prayed over it, trusting that God knew what was best for me.

Even if it feels silly to you, start praying for your husband-to-be. I used to pray that God would draw my future husband to Jesus. I prayed that God would keep him from harm as well as from doing things he'd later regret. You may not know who your man is, but God does, and he can handle answering a prayer about someone whose name you don't know yet.

TIPS FOR SEEKING ONGOING DIVINE INTERVENTION

- Create a "prayer corner" in your home for daily Bible reading and prayer.

- Use a journal to record your thoughts, fears, desires, concerns, and victories.

- Talk to God about every concern in your life (it's called prayer!).

- Be persistent in your requests.[6]

- Memorize Scripture verses to deepen your knowledge of God.

- Verbally thank God for every answered prayer, no matter how small.

Even if you don't get the answer you want right away, you can trust that God hears you and has your best interests at heart. I look at it this way. My husband and I have been blessed with two precious children: Matthew, age four and a half, and Katie, age three. We would like nothing more than to give them everything they want. But that wouldn't be in their best interests, would it? Many of their requests are dangerous, unhealthy, or both! So because we love them, we hear their requests, and then sometimes we say no.

Then there are those frustrating times when we say yes, and they continue to fuss! One sunny day Matthew wanted to go to the zoo. So we loaded up his sister and a neighbor's son and headed off to see the animals. But Matthew didn't understand that the zoo was thirty minutes away. He wanted to be there immediately. "Right now!" he demanded. "Right now, Mom. I want to go right now!" He didn't realize I was giving him his dream—but first I had to drive through our neighborhood, get on the freeway, go through town, and turn into the zoo parking lot.

We're often like little Matthew, don't you think? We want something from our heavenly Father (like a husband), and we want it *now*! We don't realize there may be a process involved in bringing our dream to pass. The next time you want to freak out because you think God is not answering your prayer, remember what 1 John 5:14–15 says: "This is the confidence (the assurance, the privilege of boldness) which we have in Him: [we are sure] that if we ask any-thing (make any request) according to His will (in agreement with His own plan), He listens to *and* hears us. And if (since) we [posi-tively] know that He listens to us in whatever we ask, we also know [with settled and absolute knowledge] that we have [granted us as our present possessions] the requests made of Him" (AMP).

Don't be like Matthew. Trust that God is at work on your behalf and thank him, even when your destination is not yet in view. God answers prayer every time we pray! I know that's hard to grasp, since we don't get a voice on our answering machine or an e-mail saying, *Yes, Victorya, I heard you. Here's the answer for request number 10,024.* God doesn't choose to answer us like that; but he does answer through circumstances, by impressing his thoughts into our minds or by caus-ing someone to come into our lives and meet our need.

Jesus said in John 15:7–8, "If you remain in me and my words re-main in you, ask whatever you wish, and it will be given you. This is to my Father's glory." Although God's timing is rarely our timing, I believe the Bible. If we love God and choose to follow him, he *will* give us the desires of our heart. That means that unless your desire for a husband vanishes from your life, God most likely has someone wonderful he is preparing for you. Trust God and hang in there!

The Right Timing

I can tell you all the secrets in the world to finding your ideal man. Ultimately, however, even after you do everything "right," the mat-ter comes down to *God's perfect timing.* Oh, we can force God's hand and settle for less than best; but if you want to marry the very best man in this world for you—the one God has purposely, perfectly prepared—then seek divine intervention and allow God to bring a husband into your life in his timing, not yours.

God's timing is different for every woman. For me, God's perfect timing for marriage was in my thirties. For my cousin, it was in her teens. For my sister, in her twenties. God had a unique plan for each of us. And all three of us have wonderful Christian husbands.

The truth is, if God had brought my husband any earlier, it would have been too soon. Will and I have more than seven years' difference between us. We often joke that if we had met sooner, it would have been illegal! Besides, I needed the time to conquer my career, graduate from seminary, and become the speaker and author God intended for me to be. My entire waiting game was about preparation.

So is yours.

Don't panic! Not everyone will have to wait until her thirties to get married like I did. (Some may have to wait longer.) If you do have to wait longer than you ever thought you would, I can assure you that the man God finally brings into your life will have been worth the wait.

only god knows

I ran into an old friend at a conference. Sue plopped down on the couch and responded with a heavy sigh when I asked, "So what's happening in your life?"

Sue wants nothing more than to marry a wonderful, godly man. She was not a believer during her first marriage. In fact, it was her divorce that ultimately brought her to her knees to find God. Ten years have passed since then, but Sue hasn't wasted one day. Since accepting Jesus as her personal Savior, she has started a new career and finished her master's degree. She keeps living life and enjoying each moment as best she can. But like all of us, she gets overwhelmed sometimes.

"Oh, Victorya," she said, "if only I knew *if* and *when* my man will appear, then I could happily continue on my way."

As I listened to my friend, I just melted. I remembered that yearning ache. No, I don't know the future or God's timing for Sue. But I know God cares. He has not forgotten her. And he has not forgotten *you*.

We'd all like God to map out the road to our future, like the AAA Auto Club or MapQuest.com. What if you knew you'd find your ideal husband and walk down the aisle three years, three weeks, and three days from now? *That would make my wait a little easier, and I could get on with my life,* you're probably thinking.

But maybe knowing the future wouldn't be such a great thing. You would know the good stuff that's ahead—but you'd know the bad stuff too. Bad things are a part of life. Would you really want to know the inevitable tragedies that lie ahead? If I had known at the age of eighteen, twenty-one, or even thirty that I'd be thirty-four before I finally got married, I truly think I would have been shattered. It was better for me to hold on to the hope over those years that my mate would appear at any moment.

Life, I've learned, is to be lived by faith and built on experience. As Romans 8:24–25 says, "Hope that is seen is no hope at all. Who hopes for what he already has? But if we hope for what we do not yet have, we wait for it patiently." Don't put your life on hold because you don't *know* what will be. Keep moving. Keep hoping. And keep waiting. God loves you, and he hasn't forgotten you.

My grandmother lived a wonderful eighty-eight years before I flew home for her funeral in Southern California. I spent a lot of time that week driving Grandpa around in my rental car. The car itself turned out to be a wonderful distraction for Grandpa, since it came equipped with one of those fun new contraptions called a GPS (Global Positioning Satellite). Grandpa had never seen one before, and he was fascinated. For several days I took him on errands, following the directions of the GPS as it told us where to turn and how far we had left to go on each trip.

During dinner one evening with my parents, Grandpa made a profound statement. "It's just amazing to me," he said. "Here some little chip in this car is signaling a satellite thousands of miles in the air, so that it knows exactly where we are in the midst of millions of people—even when we go under an overpass or turn left, right, or wrong." Then he paused and observed, "If a man-made device can know that many details about me, I finally understand how big God is and how he can see all of us at every moment."

Obviously, for a GPS to work, you must flip the On switch; otherwise, the satellite isn't able to give you directions. In a similar way, God won't force himself on you. Unless you flip the On switch and ask him to intervene, God—ever the Gentleman—will stay out of your life. Of course, unlike a GPS, even when you haven't asked for help, God still knows where you are. He never loses track. He's always ready and waiting for you to flip the switch.

Think about it. If a human being can make a device that knows where you are at all times, certainly the God who created you knows even more! And isn't that what you want, what any of us really wants? To be truly known and deeply loved?

He Was There All Along

Take out your journal and turn to the autobiography you started in secret 2. We are about to add some very important pages. I want you to go over each memory you wrote down and look more closely to see where God was during each phase of your life. You truly will be blessed as you discover that God has been involved in the details of your life all along! As you look back, answer the following questions, and you will see that God has been directing your steps—even *before* you called on him. Ask yourself:

1. What was your life like before you met God?

2. When did you meet God?

3. What has your life been like since you asked God to intervene?

4. How did you view God during a particular period, and what role did you see God playing in your life at that time?

5. What role was he actually playing?

HISTORY CAN REPEAT ITSELF!

From this day forward, invite God to intervene in your husband search. I am living proof that it works! I wrote this entry in my journal on April 9, 1996. Little did I know I had already met my husband three months earlier. We met again six months later, and the rest is history:

I'm thirty-two now. I'm still single. And for the first time in my life, without bursting into tears, I can say that perhaps God doesn't plan for me to marry. He may, but at the moment it doesn't look like it. I've heard everything you can imagine from well-meaning family and friends. And though they mean well, nothing they say comforts. "Stop looking, then God will bring the guy to you," they say. Well, I've got to tell you, I have done everything in my human power, including intense periods of prayer, to find my husband. I think relatives have even fasted. And still God has not brought Mr. Right along. But what he has done is be faithful to me throughout my life. He has rescued me from damaging relationships. He has always been there for me no matter what, and I am happy. . . . I still believe it's better to be single and alone then married and lonely.

If you're stuck in the waiting game right now, seek divine intervention. You won't find a more interested ally. God has promised to give you the desires of your heart. If you allow him, he will put the right desires in your heart and remove the wrong ones. If God has called you to be single forever, he will change your heart to happily accept it. Otherwise, stay alert! Your man worth keeping is on the way.

BE A
GREAT
Date

Few classes on dating etiquette existed when I was single, but books were plentiful. I read nearly every book published on the subject. In fact, over the years I scoured, devoured, and analyzed the advice of untold numbers of psychiatrists, counselors, pastors, and bachelors-turned-authors. And my, oh my, how they contradicted one another! Early on, it became quite clear to me that just because something is in print doesn't mean it's accurate or wise counsel. Some books contained gems; others, rubble; most, a combination of the two. I tried to put into practice the good and discard the bad.

Through all my personal trials and errors, hits and misses, I earned my stripes as my own dating expert. I went out with well over a hundred men during my midtwenties to early thirties. I dated poor guys and rich ones. I dated doctors, lawyers, and bankers; actors, models, and producers; firemen, cops, and pilots; politicians, preachers, and singers. You name an occupation, and I'm sure I dated a man in that field.

Of all those men, amazingly, only three failed to ask me for a second date. I have first-date etiquette down to a science! And now I'm about to teach it to *you*.

Consider this secret your Dating 101 class. The best of the best dating manuals. Your very own crash course in the fine art of dating, with special emphasis on first dates and obtaining that ever-important second date. Have you ever gone on a dream date, only to wonder why Mr. Perfect never called again? Here's your chance to see what you may have done wrong—and learn how to get it right the next time.

We're about to cover everything from what to say to what to wear to when, if ever, you should offer to pay for dinner or a movie. We'll even suggest some fun ideas for where to go and what to do (in case your date makes the mistake of showing up without a plan). I assure you, if you put into practice what I'm going to reveal in this secret, you will dramatically increase your repeat-date ratio.

CALLS, CLOTHES, AND CONFIDENCE

As I've said before, I believe that men should always be allowed to lead in a romantic relationship. When you do the pursuing, you never know for sure if the man likes you or if he is agreeing to get together for lack of a better offer. But when the man makes the first move and asks for a date, at least you know he is interested in considering a romantic future as opposed to a platonic friendship. So let the man lead, and avoid needless embarrassment and heartache.

This principle applies not just to dates but to initiating phone calls too. Let *him* call *you*. In the early stages of a relationship, don't call a guy unless you are returning his call. What if a man gives you his number instead of asking for yours? Kindly reply, "Oh, I'm not comfortable with calling guys. Here's my number if you'd like to chat." If his motivation in offering his phone number was fear of rejection, he now knows you will respond favorably to his call. If he was only interested in stroking his ego by hearing your voice on his answering machine, you're better off without him.

Let's consider the positive scenario: The phone rings, and you hear a male voice on the line. When the guy identifies himself, don't make the mistake of acting aloof or pretending you don't know who he is. Say something like, "Hi, it's great to hear from you," or, "Cathy said you would call." If he asks about your day, and it's been your absolute worst, don't overwhelm him with negativity; say something light, such as, "It's better *now*." Be warm, friendly, and likable. Make talking with you *easy*.

When he brings up the suggestion of a date, say, "Yes, I'd like that" or, "I'd love to get together with you." You're not desperate; you're not ecstatic. You simply think that a date would be a pleasant experience, and you're looking forward to it. Convey *that* kind of message with your words and tone, not, "Oh, thank God! I haven't had a date in six months! You just saved my life!"

phone call Rules

In 1996 a popular dating book called *The Rules* reached the top of the *New York Times* bestseller list shortly after the authors appeared on *The Oprah Winfrey Show*. In the book, Ellen Fein and Sherrie Schneider offered thirty-five "time-tested secrets" for catching a man. Some of their advice was great; but some, I must say, bordered on the ridiculous. I wasn't surprised to hear that one of the authors divorced a few years later, since she had written so much about clever game playing and so little about developing a real relationship.

Some of Fein and Schneider's better advice (with a little modification) was in the area of phone calls. They had three rules:

1. Don't call him, and rarely return his calls.

2. Always end the phone call first.

3. Don't accept a Saturday night date after Wednesday.[1]

I have a little problem with the first rule. As I've already said, I believe the man should initiate the phone calls. I think that's especially true before the two of you reach the commitment stage. But to never return his calls, as these ladies suggest, is going too far; it's game playing. They claim that if a man really wants to talk to you, he'll keep calling until he gets you on the phone. Maybe, maybe not. Remember, men are insecure too. If you don't return his calls, why wouldn't he just assume you're not interested, lick his wounds, and move on? Besides, do you really want to spend your time sitting next to the phone, praying for his next call attempt?

I think the theory behind the second rule—"Always end the phone call first"—has merit. Don't bore the guy until all he can think of is how to get off the phone. We women love to talk details. Save them for your girlfriends! But I *would* modify the rule this way: Don't focus too hard on trying to be the first one to jump off every phone call. Pay attention to how his side of the conversation is going. When he starts to fade, politely tell him, "It was great chatting, but I've got to run."

The third rule—"Don't accept a Saturday night date after Wednesday"—is pretty smart as it is. Here's why: If a man asks you out at the last minute, he obviously was not greatly anticipating the opportunity to see you; otherwise, he would have secured a plan ahead of time. For all you know, other women have turned him down, and you're his last choice for the evening. By letting him know he needs to schedule dates with you earlier in the week, you send the message that you are *worth* booking early.

Don't lecture him if he calls on Friday for a Friday or Saturday date, however. Just say, "Oh, I'd love to, but I already have plans" or, "Gosh, I'm already doing something that night. Can I have a rain check?" You aren't obligated to tell him what those plans are. Maybe you're going to have dinner with your parents or stay at home and catch up on laundry. He doesn't have to know. A little bit of mystery is intriguing and desirable! And definitely don't cancel plans with a friend in order to go out with him, especially if he calls late in the week. It's rude to your friend (you need friends in your life!), and it sends him the wrong message: that all he has to do is call, and you'll drop everything. If the two of you are meant to be together, you will surely have another opportunity to go out.

But I Haven't Got a Thing to Wear

Once your man sets up the date, try to get a sense of his plans for your get-together. It's so nice to know what to wear before he shows up! You don't want to be in a floor-length gown if he's going to show up in shorts and sandals. Trust me, I had my share of dates when I had to rush back to my room to change into something more appropriate.

Whatever the dress code, make sure you choose an outfit that feels good on you. When you're uncomfortable in clothing, suddenly comfort means everything! You will have enough stress built into the evening without the added anxiety of itchy fabric, pinching toes, or too-snug pants. You may look fabulous, but you'll be self-conscious and fidgeting all night. Wouldn't you rather be gazing into his eyes?

confidence counts

Let's say you get a phone call on Monday for a date on Saturday. You think all week about what you're going to wear, and you choose the perfect outfit. Finally the weekend arrives, and the knock comes at your door.

Don't panic. You've done so much to prepare for this moment. Now it's time to relax and enjoy yourself. I know, I know—easier said than done! Would it ease your mind if I told you that everyone gets nervous before a first date, males and females alike? Even the smooth-talking types are not as calm, cool, and collected inside as they appear on the outside. So go ahead, *relax*. And if you can't relax, smile anyway. At least you'll *appear* confident. And confidence is attractive to the opposite sex.

While I now consider myself a confident woman, that wasn't always the case. It took time and practice for me to finally reach the point where I could handle an evening out without showing nervousness or intimidation. How did I do it?

I faked it until I felt it.

That's right. That's what I did in dating and in business. I walked around with my shoulders back, stomach in, head held high, and a smile on my face. I faked self-assurance even when I didn't feel it. People believed I was confident and relaxed. And you know what? Eventually I believed it myself.

Feelings follow action, not the reverse. That definitely proved true for me in my effort to move past my insecurities. Even if you are burned out on the whole dating scene, be optimistic and force yourself to relax. Feel the fear—and date anyway. Yes, I am actually saying, "Do it afraid!"

WHAT TO DO ON A FIRST DATE

Let's say your guy arrives. You smile at one another, say your hellos, grab your purse, and the date is on. Now it's time for you to put into practice *the ultimate dating secret*. It comes straight from the Bible— although I had to read it in several other places before it really sunk in. God must have wanted to make sure I mastered this principle (which I needed for both my personal and professional life), because it came up in three books I was reading during a single week. Only one was a dating book.

NOW I GET IT!

Wanting to improve my effectiveness as a Hollywood agent, I had picked up two great books on communication—Dale Carnegie's *How to Win Friends and Influence People* and Barbara Walters's *How to Talk with Practically Anybody about Practically Anything*. I was also in the middle of *Love Tactics: How to Win the One You Want*, by Thomas McKnight and Robert Phillips, one of my all-time favorite dating books.

All three books offered this same piece of biblical advice

(although they didn't necessarily tag it as such). The third time it passed my eyes, I finally had my "aha!" moment. It seemed so obvious, so logical, yet I had to read it over and over before it clicked. What is this great biblical secret I'm teasing you with? Simply this: "Everyone should be quick to listen, slow to speak and slow to become angry" (James 1:19). Once I incorporated this principle into my dating life, I behaved the same basic way on every date— genuinely interested in getting to know the man sitting across from me. I was quick to listen to his stories, slow to speak about mine, and careful not to spill out any anger over my past or present circumstances.

It sounds so simple, and it really is. Just make the first date all about him! Dale Carnegie, one of the greatest communicators of the twentieth century, wrote, "I never forgot that to be genuinely interested in other people is a most important quality. . . . One can win the attention and time and cooperation of even the most sought-after people by becoming genuinely interested in them."[2]

Get it? He talks. You listen. Make this your motto: "I already know me. I want to know you." After all, your goal for the first date is to get a second date, not to talk him right out the door and out of your life. Barbara Walters gives this advice: "Don't talk excessively about yourself at all in the beginning. Even if you're an older woman and unmarried, it doesn't require an explanation. . . . So take it easy on the personal confessions. It will come out as time goes by, when the relationship is well enough established that the skeletons in the closet will be considered amusing décor."[3]

Think of your first date as an interview. Focus on drawing out this new man. As Dale Carnegie said, "The royal road to a person's heart is to talk about the things he or she treasures most."[4] If the guy is worth seeing again, and if more dates follow, you will have plenty of time later to talk about you. This first time, get to know him. After all, people are fascinating! If you are passionate about meeting new people, you will never get bored on a date.

WHY MAKE IT ALL ABOUT HIM?

Here are some great reasons to make your first date all about him:

- You know he's interested in the topic.
- You'll seem more intriguing to him.
- You'll find out if he matches your husband wish list.
- You can relax because the focus isn't on you.
- You'll be more likely to have a second date.

Think about it. If you let your date be the topic of conversation, he will probably go away saying to himself, "Hey, I really had a great time. I want to see her again!" And at this stage, that's exactly what you want.

The Eyes Have It

Here's another tip: make your date *feel* that you're interested in him by looking directly into his eyes. I'm not talking about gazing dreamily and emoting your undying love. I'm saying, offer him your respect and appreciation for sacrificing his time to be with you— and to do that, the eyes definitely have it. Besides, focusing attentively with eye contact is just good manners!

When I was in Hollywood, I noticed that eye contact was often lacking on dates. The glitz and glamour of the movie business promotes a mentality of "see and be seen." People tend to spend more time checking out others in the room and less time looking at the person in front of them. I'm not saying you should never take your eyes off your date. If you see someone you know, say hi—but introduce your new friend too.

Even if you realize at some point during that date that you don't want to pursue a relationship, treat the guy with the same respect (read: attention) you'd like to receive. That's sound advice going back two thousand years, and it comes from the lips of Jesus himself: "In everything, therefore, treat people the same way you want them to treat you" (Matthew 7:12 NASB).

Barbara Walters has interviewed some of the world's most famous, powerful, and important people. Here's what she says about attention: "The most charming people I know give the impression that they've waited all day to speak to me alone. For the moments that we're talking, no one and nothing else is important. Even in a crowded room, we seem to have isolated ourselves."[5] You will endear yourself to others if you will just practice this tip, be it in friendship, business, or romance. So make the effort to look your date in the eyes and show him by your attention that you care.

Pardon the Interruption

Speaking of attention, it seems to me that social behavior has gone downhill with the ever-increasing popularity of cell phones. Convenience has allowed people to become downright rude these days! I'm a cell-phone addict, but that doesn't mean I should answer the phone every time it rings or suddenly interrupt a visit with someone in order to place a quick call "before I forget." Every time you take or make a cell phone call in the presence of someone else, you make it clear that the person on the phone is more important than the person in front of you.

If your phone rings again and again throughout the course of your date, it will be an attention stealer—no matter how sincerely or how often you apologize for it. If you have a cell phone, I assume you also have a silent ring option, voice mail, and most likely, caller ID to identify the incoming caller. Use them! If you want to win the heart of a man worth keeping, leave your phone in your purse, put it on Silent, and think twice before taking it out. Unless there's some kind of emergency, give your date the respect of your focused attention.

THE ART OF CONVERSATION

On a first date, it's always good to begin your conversation with safe, nonpersonal subjects, such as the weather, music, the surrounding scenery, or mutual acquaintances. Starting with such topics—also known as small talk—gives both of you a chance to adjust to one another's "vibe." As Barbara Walters puts it, "A warm-up period of small talk between strangers gives each time to make those mysterious little adaptations that result in what we then call being on the same wavelength."[6]

As you both begin feeling comfortable, *then* you can steer the conversation toward your date and his interests. Sure, you can interject information about yourself occasionally; but do so briefly, and only to show that you have things in common. Then go right back to asking questions about him. Keeping your date in the spotlight keeps him invested in the evening while nonverbally defining you as intriguing. *Bingo!*

In *Love Tactics: How to Win the One You Want*, Thomas McKnight and Robert Phillips give this advice: "If the other person asks you some sincere questions about yourself, answer them without getting carried away. Remember that their interest has its limits. In the early stages, especially, you only want to reveal enough about yourself to whet their appetite and make them want to know more! Always maintain some mystery about yourself. This will keep them coming back around."[7]

Whatever you do, don't use a question from your date as an opening to talk about your last heartbreak. No one wants to hear you whine all night. What he'll really be thinking is, *What did her ex know that I don't know?* And don't expose a history of credit-card debt, job-hopping, speeding tickets and car wrecks, or plain ol' pessimism about love. Believe me, that's way too much information (TMI, as I call it) for a first date. We all have baggage. It is much safer sharing such things down the line, after the friendship has grown.

Stick to asking questions. If you listen to his responses and let the conversation naturally lead to the next inquiry, you'll avoid long, awkward moments of silence. Not that every moment needs to be filled with chatter; sometimes silence is nice for collecting your thoughts. Just don't get so focused on coming up with questions that you forget to listen to the answers. Don't pretend to be listening; *really listen.*

Who knows? Even if you don't feel attracted to your date at first, you might change your mind as you get to know him. I mean, think back over some of the people you've cared about in your life. Didn't they become more intriguing once you learned about their lives, interests, careers, and past experiences? Your date may grow on you too!

And remember, practice makes perfect. Don't feel bad if you come across a bit rigid or rehearsed the first few times you try this interview technique. If your date calls you on it and says, "Hey, are you interviewing me for a job or something?" just laugh and say, "No, I'm sorry. I guess I'm asking a lot of questions, huh? I'm just interested in getting to know you. I hope I'm not offending you."

Keep reminding yourself that this is a date, not an interrogation. You're just spending time getting to know someone you find interesting!

Tell me About the Time . . .

Does the idea of keeping a conversation moving by asking questions make you nervous? You can make it easier on yourself by being prepared. Take a few moments right now to pull out your husband wish list and remind yourself of the qualities you are looking for in a man worth keeping. Now turn those qualities into a list of questions you can build upon to discover if your date is a match. Write them on the next page in your journal. Come up with about twenty questions that you can review and keep fresh in your mind before your date picks you up.

Here are some you may want to pursue:

1. Where did you grow up?

2. Tell me about your childhood.

3. Tell me about your family. How many siblings do you have? Are your parents still together? Do you get along?

4. Did you attend college?

5. When did you move out on your own?

6. Did you always know you wanted to pursue the career you're in now?

7. What are your dreams for the future?

8. What is your spiritual background? Did you go to church when you were young? Have you made a personal decision about Jesus?

9. Do you see yourself as a husband and father? Do either of those roles scare you?

Some of these questions are pretty heavy hitting, I know. You'll want to start with lighter questions to help warm up the evening. I put these next ones in the "small talk" category. A few good warmup questions might include:

1. What are your favorite sports or hobbies?

2. What do you like to do in your spare time?

3. What kind of music do you like?

4. What's your favorite food?

5. What movies have you seen lately?

6. Any favorite TV shows?

7. If you could live anywhere, where would it be?

8. What's your favorite vacation spot?

Does it seem manipulative to come up with a list of questions for your date? Do you think interviewing him is tantamount to acting?

Don't worry; it's not. This is important, real-life stuff! You need to draw out vital information about your date early on, *before* the chemistry between you starts to dominate your thinking. He may be gorgeous and make your heart go all aflutter. But if he has no interest in marriage and hates his mom (negative feelings about women—especially Mom—are a major red flag), you'd do best to cut your losses long before the first kiss.

Flattery Will Get You Everywhere

As the evening progresses and you learn things that impress you about your date, flatter him. That's right! Sincere flattery is a good thing. The intent is to make him feel admired for who he is. So be genuine and specific with your praise. For example, if you think your guy is the best-looking person you have ever seen, don't make a blanket statement about him being handsome. Compliment the feature you admire most. ("Your eyes are the most amazing shade of blue.") If he scaled a tall mountain or fought off a wild animal, compliment his bravery.

Even if he brushes off or downplays your words, rest assured, he loves them! The authors of *Love Tactics* write:

> When people seem disbelieving of, and resistant to, your flattery, realize that it's just a show on their part. Actually, they are deeply affected by it—more than they'd like you to know. The human need for appreciation is stronger than any human ability to resist it. A word of caution though, flattery is very potent, like fine perfume. A little bit goes a long way. . . . Too much flattery may cause your praise to appear unduly suspicious and undermine your genuine sincerity.[8]

Sincere flattery in small amounts will add warmth to your time together. So will occasionally touching your date's arm or hand as you make a point. Remember, the goal is to be the one pursued, not the pursuer; so be sure to keep your touch light and brief. You are not initiating snuggling, kissing, or embracing. You are just being warm (and flirting a little) by offering the attention of a brief touch.

The bottom line is, you will get a lot further into a man's heart on a first date if you keep the focus on him and show, not tell, your feelings. So zip those lips; offer an occasional, brief touch; laugh at the appropriate moments; look directly into his eyes; and don't forget to smile. And when he asks you for a second date, don't look so surprised!

DUTCH TREAT, ANYONE?

I often get asked, "Is it OK to go 'Dutch treat'?"—that is, is it OK for a woman to pay her own way on a date? Absolutely not! A lady should never go "Dutch treat" on a romantic date, period. Friends go Dutch. You are not looking for just another friend. Besides, do you really want a man who isn't willing to pamper you? No matter how competent you are, no matter what salary you make, you want a strong man who can take care of you physically and financially, no? If you go Dutch treat—or worse, pick up the entire tab yourself—you send one of two messages: that you are the one in control or that you are not worthy of being taken care of. Snap out of that attitude immediately!

On a first date, the guy should always pay. Later on, as the relationship develops, you can reciprocate (perhaps every third or fourth date) by footing the bill for an inexpensive evening or cooking at your place. Just don't outdo your date to the point that he thinks he owes you. That will work against your goal of winning his heart. You want him to think *he's* captured *your* heart, not the reverse.

In *The Rules* by Ellen Fein and Sherrie Schneider, the authors recommend not only letting the guy pay but also never meeting him halfway. They believe your date needs to make every effort to accommodate you as a show of his extreme interest in winning you over.[9] As with Fein and Schneider's phone rules, however, I think this rule needs a little modification. Many times on a first date I was more comfortable meeting the guy somewhere rather than being picked up at my home. I'm sure I never undermined my date's sense of conquest by meeting him at a restaurant or movie theater halfway between our neighborhoods.

"But wait!" you may protest. "Forget technicalities like meeting halfway. What if my date simply doesn't have any money?"

Let him be creative. You are a prize worth winning! He ought to show *some* effort toward winning you over, don't you think? He can take you on a hike in the park, a tour through a museum, a walk on the beach, or a scenic bike ride around a lake. Let him come up with something fun and interesting that stays within his budget. Even a poor college student can scrape together enough money for a picnic of fried chicken and coleslaw. Some of the most romantic dates I ever went on were free or inexpensive for the man.

The point is, if a guy really wants to win you, he'll figure it out on his own. Don't throw yourself at him, offer to pay, and take the challenge away. It's in a man's nature to fight for what he wants. Besides, something not earned is rarely appreciated.

when All Else Fails, go to plan B

I was never impressed when my date showed up without a plan, but it occasionally happened. Experience taught me to have a Plan B in mind, just in case. (After the newness of a relationship wears off, ladies, you'll find your Plan B becomes more and more the norm. Men seem to relax on planning once the quest for your heart is over.)

So stop for a moment and pull out your journal again. Think about the restaurants in your area and make a list of at least six of your favorites: two that are inexpensive, casual, and fun; two that are moderately priced with a hip atmosphere or intriguing theme; and two that are romantic but pricey, perhaps with an incredible view. Make a note if reservations are required.

Now turn the page in your journal and think of some fun things you'd like to do on a date. Categorize these activities according to price range, as you did with the restaurants. Some good ideas might be church and brunch; a trip to the beach or nearby hiking trail; bicycling or rollerblading; dinner and a movie; a visit to a museum, amusement park, or local tourist trap; a concert, play, or sporting event. As you can see, this list includes a variety of free, moderately priced, and expensive activities.

Be prepared—but don't advertise your Plan B when your date walks in the door. In fact, only bring it up if he specifically asks, "Um, what do you want to do?" Let *him* make the effort for the evening. Hopefully, he will have done so in advance. Your preparation is only for a worst-case scenario.

If asked, though, be sensitive to your date's financial status before offering your plan. (You can sometimes get a clue from his job or his car.) If he's a starving college student without a trust fund, don't suggest lobster at a posh restaurant overlooking the ocean. Generally speaking, it's really best not to recommend the expensive restaurants or activities unless he makes it clear that's what he's looking for. It's his wallet, not yours.

Once you're on your way, let him take the lead again. Allow him to open doors for you or pull out your chair, if he'd like. Chivalry is not dead. It's alive and well if you let it be. Think Scarlett O'Hara, and let your date pamper you. You are a prize worth winning, and you deserve it!

At the end of the evening, give him a moment to initiate the good-bye. If you feel uncomfortable or awkward, or just want to get the evening over with, do what I used to do: initiate a hug and maybe a peck on the cheek, and say, "Thank you for a nice evening." You're not being overtly forward or physical. You can hug someone you are not romantically drawn to! I always preferred a hug to a handshake; handshakes felt more business than social.

I assure you, if you put the principles in this secret into practice, you will dramatically increase your repeat-date ratio. And if you live by Jesus's words, "Treat people the same way you want them to treat you," you will sleep well knowing that you have done well, no matter the end result.

If your date doesn't call back, he obviously wasn't the one for you. Don't sweat it. Head up, shoulders back. Look forward to the future and say, "Next!"

QUICK TIPS FOR A
GREAT FIRST DATE

- Relax—and if you can't relax, fake it.

- Wear a comfy outfit.

- Allow him the opportunity to impress you by letting him take the lead.

- Look him in the eye.

- Smile.

- Ask questions.

- Flatter him sincerely.

- Make the date all about him.

DON'T
FREAK
Him Out

You've had your first date. It seemed to go well. Now he's called and asked you to go out again. Your head is spinning! Wow, isn't this the most amazing feeling you've ever had? You're sure nothing and no one has ever made you feel this good!

I have to tell you, next to your wedding day and the birth of your children, no time in your life feels better than those early days of new love. You walk about ten pounds lighter. Your face glows. Friends and family notice the change in you.

You are infatuated.

"No, no, it's more than that," you argue. "I'm in love."

It couldn't be love—yet. No one can fall in permanent love overnight. Your feelings of being "in love" are a combination of chemistry, lust, and emotions that have exploded within you. I'm not discounting your experience or trying to squash your dreams of a future with this man. Enjoy every moment! Those feelings of bliss don't last forever, even if you've found your man worth keeping. Not that you can't be in love forever; of course you can. It's just those walking-on-clouds, goose-bump feelings that won't endure. So go ahead. Recognize your elation for what it is, and enjoy it!

Have you noticed another feeling competing with your bliss, though? A strange emotion lurking just beneath the surface of your euphoria? I'll tell you what it is: terror. It's the fear that you'll wake up to find out you've been dreaming—or that he'll wake up and wise up.

What do you do with this combination of infatuation and fear, knowing that the next date is just around the corner?

Don't freak out.

And whatever you do, don't freak *him* out.

Here's your mission: to inspire this man to continue seeing you while you decide if he's a keeper. How do you do that? You keep your head, no matter how high you've soared into the clouds. Take it slowly, even if this is the first time in your life you've felt so strongly about a man. Refrain from advertising your feelings before he is ready to reveal his.

WHAT'S YOUR HURRY?

Almost every time I tell an infatuated, starry-eyed young lady to take it slowly with her new love, she comes up with an example of someone she knows who met and married her spouse in five days (or thirty days). Fine. For every argument you can find an exception. But I promise you, even rushed romances that eventually go the distance reach a point where the emotional bliss dissipates, and both parties wake up wondering, "Who *is* this person?" Your goal is to find out that information *before* you commit your heart to a man, or worse, your signature to a marriage license.

You can feel deeply about a man early on; but understand, those feelings are based on your perception of who you *think* he is. It takes time to find out if his promise matches his reality.

I've heard the stages of love described many ways. My favorite description is by Tim Timmons and Charlie Hedges. They boil courtship down to four words: *hoping, scoping, coping,* and *roping.*[1] Doesn't that just capture the whole concept? You meet someone and *hope* this might be "the one." Then you spend time *scoping* your man to see if he's as wonderful as he seems. Next you work to secure and further develop a committed relationship as you face one another's differences. (That's the *coping* part.) And finally, you *rope* your man by walking down the aisle of matrimony and beginning a new life together.

Every relationship goes through stages, however you term them. Eventually you reach a crossroads, and you either walk away or walk the aisle. But the beginning is always a fairy-tale state of bliss. Your Prince Charming can do no wrong. *How did I get so lucky?* you ask yourself often. At this stage, even your man's annoying traits seem adorable and endearing. Scales of euphoria blind you to any blatant faults that are readily visible to the rest of the world.

That's precisely why you must take a gradual approach: It will take time for you to discover this person's true self. And it will take time for true feelings—based on reality, not infatuation—to develop between you.

once or twice a week

So how do you plod along at a tortoise pace when you are overwhelmed with emotion? Make a pact with yourself to only see your new guy once or twice a week for the first month. Work up to three of four times a week (only if he requests it) by the third month.

Wow, that's not a lot of time together, is it?

Exactly.

If he calls you every day and wants to talk on the phone for hours, or he e-mails you constantly, great. But don't accept in-person dates more often than this formula prescribes. Why? First, it will help both of you keep your passion under control. (For more on this subject, see the next secret, "Know Your Limits.") Second, he won't get the opportunity to tire of you before he falls deeply in love. The last thing you want to do is drown a potentially great relationship by "pouring it on" too thick in the beginning.

It's just a fact of nature: Too much too soon of *anything* produces negative results. If too much rain falls overnight, the town will flood. If you lay out in the sun too long on the first day of summer, you'll get a sunburn. If you eat too much food too quickly, you'll get sick. (Ever watch a hot dog–eating contest?) As a wise man once said, "If you find honey, eat just enough—too much of it, and you will vomit. Seldom set foot in your neighbor's house—too much of you, and he will hate you" (Proverbs 25:16–17).

Love, like a skyscraper, needs a foundation. Otherwise, when the storms of life come (and they *will* come), your relationship will not be strong enough to survive.

Don't tell your guy what you are doing. Just keep an eye on your calendar. If he requests to see you more than twice a week the first month or more than four times a week by the third month, kindly tell him you'd love to but you're busy. If you have been living out secrets 1 through 6, you're not game playing, and you're not lying. You *do* have an active life with a busy calendar. You're simply guarding your heart and his—although it's best to keep that to yourself for now.

men Are Like Frogs

Ever heard the best way to cook a frog? You place him in a pot of lukewarm water, turn on the burner, and let the water gradually heat to a boil. The frog is slowly, almost comfortably, cooked by surprise. He doesn't notice the incremental increase in temperature, so he doesn't think to jump out of the pot and save his life. If the pot is boiling from the start, however, he will hop out the moment his little green toe touches the water.

This illustration puts a new spin on the "men are frogs" concept. No doubt you've heard the traditional axiom that you have to kiss a lot of frogs to find your prince. That may be true. But here's another way to look at it: men are like frogs in that you need to keep them feeling comfortable in the pot while you gradually turn up the heat. Your goal is to allow your guy plenty of time to fall in love so that eventually he'll be too far gone to jump out and run away.

When you think you've met the man of your dreams, don't rush to advertise your feelings. Act like you care. Respond to his lead. But don't be the first to reveal your love with words, gifts, letters, or e-mail. Too many girls scare away great guys by professing their undying love and devotion too early. Let him suspect you are falling hard by the way you look at him or your eagerness to accept his date requests—but no vocal or written confirmations yet, please. The minute you verbally admit you're in love, he perceives your words to mean he's obligated "from this day forward" to take care of you and keep you happy. If he's not ready for that commitment, you have just officially freaked him out.

So what if you begin dating a guy who tries to gobble up your calendar 24/7? Certainly he's not a bad person for wanting to see you all the time. But you can't let him! Even a man worth keeping can be oblivious to the fact that he will tire of you if he is allowed to see too much of you in the beginning. It's up to you to be the strong one and just say no. There's too much at stake. If you cave in and see him at his every whim, over time he's likely to grow bored, pull back, call less, or suddenly find himself "swamped" at work. You'll be left wondering what went wrong.

DATING DON'TS

Mike is so like many guys I know. If he's pursuing a girl and she announces her love early on, he gets scared off, afraid she thinks he's something he's not. But if she doesn't vocalize her feelings, he keeps chasing.

Recently Mike began dating Holly, a woman who impressed me with her instinct to play it cool. For the first month or two, things seemed to go well between them, and they saw each other regularly. Then Mike began calling less frequently. A summer holiday approached, and Mike didn't call Holly in the five days preceding the weekend. Didn't he want to spend the holiday with her? Holly was disappointed and wondered what was going on.

But here's what Holly did right at this point that many girls do wrong: She didn't call Mike—even though her mom was going to be in town that weekend, and she had wanted to use the occasion to introduce the two of them. Nor did she scold, lecture, pout, or punish when Mike called a full week later. She was simply happy to hear his voice.

As it turned out, Mike was having a panic spell, thinking things were getting too close too soon. Because Holly didn't press him, however, the feelings of panic passed, and he was able to retest the waters when he was ready. What if she had called and pushed him to get together that holiday? He probably would have thought, *I was right to back off. She wants something I'm not ready for.* Instead he thought, *Wow, I guess I was wrong. Holly could be the one for me.* So here's the first dating don't:

DON'T FREAK OUT (OR FREAK HIM OUT)

Don't freak out your man during the first few months of dating! If he seems to pull back or doesn't call when you expect him to, he may be fighting his feelings. Let him work them out in his own time. He may have a few loose ends to tie up in his life or other relationships. He may *genuinely* be on a major deadline at work. You just don't know everything going on in his life yet.

So don't panic or push. He will pursue you full-force right up until the moment he feels obligated. Even if you do everything right and play it cool, when he begins to feel a sense of obligation, he will pull back a bit—not necessarily because of anything you said or did, not because he doesn't have feelings for you, but simply because he's terrified of losing his freedom. Your job is to prevent him from feeling that way for as long as you possibly can. For a man to fall in love completely, he must think he's done so freely and willingly (even if he doesn't realize what hit him).

So hang in there and don't call if he seems to vanish from your life for a while. Waiting may be torture, but it's not as bad as the heartbreak you'll experience if you push for attention when he's begging for space. Let him pull back and miss you. When he finally calls again, just move forward without skipping a beat. You will calm his fears and gain his trust if you don't freak out. And don't worry. If he's the one for you, like Arnold Schwarzenegger he *will* be back.

Let's take a look at five more dating "don'ts."

Don't Scold Him

If the man you're dating acts disrespectfully, tell him. But being disrespectful and not calling for a while are two different things. Don't scold him because you feel he's not reciprocating your feelings. The only time you have a right to scold him is when he's being blatantly disrespectful or rude. I assume you would scold anyone in your life who exhibited such behavior.

Don't Accept Last-Minute Dates

We mentioned this in the last secret, but let's take a moment to reiterate the point. When you accept last-minute dates in the first few months of dating, you teach your guy bad habits. You want him to anticipate his time with you; if he's booking at the last minute, that means he hasn't been pining away for you all week. It may also mean one of three things, none of which are good: he's also dating someone else who is higher on his priority list, he has a controlling personality and thinks your plans don't count, or he's taking advantage of you, knowing that all he has to do is call and you'll drop everything to see him.

DON'T BUY HIM EXPENSIVE GIFTS

It is perfectly fine for *him* to pamper *you*. That's how it should be. Let your guy win you over, not the reverse. In fact, you can be assured he is actively pursuing you if you feel slightly indebted to him. You just don't want him to think he owes you! That's why you should never buy him expensive gifts or try to match or better any gifts he gives you. I'm not saying you can never give your man a gift. Just don't go overboard. If he is not serious about you yet, an expensive gift will make him feel pressured. If he's into you but can't afford to reciprocate, he'll feel intimidated and pull away.

DON'T MAKE HIM PAY ALL THE TIME

In the last secret, we said you should never go Dutch or pay your own way on a first date. As your relationship progresses, however, it's a nice gesture to occasionally cook your guy a meal, pick up the tab at a restaurant, or pay for dessert or coffee if you go somewhere after a movie. How often should you do this? Nothing is etched in stone, but every third or fourth date is probably a good rule of thumb. By occasionally cooking for your man or paying for all or part of a date, you're offering a token of appreciation for how much he pampers you the rest of the time. You're not outdoing him. You're just showing him that you're a giving person, not someone who is always taking.

DON'T BE HIS THERAPIST

Many women mistakenly feel that if they listen to all the details of their guy's last relationship, he will fall madly in love with them for being so understanding. Wrong! Don't be your date's therapist, and don't let him be yours. You want him to be focusing on his new life with you, not his old life with someone else. I learned this one the hard way. As I've told you earlier, every guy I ever "fixed" left me soon after and married the next girl he dated!

SIX QUICK DATING DON'TS

- Don't freak out (or freak him out).
- Don't scold him.
- Don't accept last-minute dates.
- Don't buy him expensive gifts.
- Don't make him pay all the time.
- Don't be his therapist.

THE LONG–DISTANCE RELATIONSHIP

Long-distance relationships are unique and worthy of a few words here. I have been in my share of long-distance relationships, living anywhere from fifty to two thousand miles away from the guy I was dating. The plus side of this kind of relationship is that passion is more manageable since you're not face to face as often as you would be if you lived in the same town. Plus, you spend so much time phoning and e-mailing that you really get to know all about each other. The risk, however, is that you may fall in love with the guy's mind and not have chemistry when you are together.

How can you find out if the man in your long-distance relationship is worth keeping? Stick to my secret of letting the man do the pursuing, with one modification. When he comes to town to see you, go ahead and clear your calendar so you can make up for lost time. Your friends will understand since they get to spend lots of time with you when he's not around.

How often should you travel to see one another? Let him take the lead on that decision. The basic rules still apply—although it's a good idea for you to start saving up vacation time at work so you can take days off when he comes to visit. If you want to take turns paying for your airfare when you travel to see him, that's OK, but allow him to pay for most everything else.

When my husband and I began dating, he lived in Oklahoma City and I lived in Los Angeles. I had accumulated four weeks of vacation time at work. Rather than use it a week at a time, however, I took off a few days here and there, stringing together many long three- or four-day weekends. As a result, during our eighteen-month courtship, Will and I spent every holiday plus well over a dozen long weekends together. We saw each other on average once every three weeks. When I visited him in Oklahoma City, we took turns paying for my airfare, but he covered all other expenses.

Be careful not to escalate your long-distance romance too soon. But if things do turn serious, let the guy be the one to decide to move to your town or ask you to move to his. Be aware that if you choose to move in order to explore your future with this man, you will be uprooting your entire life—friends, family, job, and church. If the relationship doesn't work out, you'll be starting over on every front. Because of my career, I chose not to move to Oklahoma City until *after* our wedding. Leaving Los Angeles meant I had to retire from the entertainment business. But Will was definitely my man worth keeping, so I did it gladly—and I've never regretted the sacrifice.

GUY BUDDIES AND GIRL FRIENDS

For two years Thomas and Maggie were best friends. Maggie called Thomas several times a week, and he always listened intently to her life sagas. When weekends rolled around, he often agreed to catch a movie, share a ride to church, or join her at a party. Throughout their friendship, though, every call and every meeting was at Maggie's initiative. Thomas never dialed her number unless he was returning her call. They never kissed; he never even tried. Maggie rationalized that he just respected her too much to "go there."

You can imagine Maggie's devastation when, out of the blue, Thomas stopped returning her calls as quickly as he used to. Suddenly his schedule was always filled up on the weekends. It wasn't long before some mutual friends asked Maggie what she thought of Thomas's "new love." When she pranced over to his house to confront him, Thomas admitted he had fallen in love with someone and hadn't known how to tell Maggie.

"But I didn't lead you on," he asserted. "We were never dating. I never asked you out, kissed you, or professed anything more than friendship."

Well, Thomas may not have thought they were dating, but Maggie did. It took her years to get over him.

The "buddy syndrome" can happen anywhere, but it's particularly epidemic in the church. Single Christian women frequently pursue friendships with Christian guys and then ask these "buddies" to accompany them to movies, concerts, and group activities. Here's the problem: when the lady initiates the relationship, nine times out of ten, the man is not romantically interested. His feelings are platonic. She is in love.

He doesn't intend to lead her on. He may not even realize she likes him "that way." But the more time they spend together, the deeper she falls. It doesn't matter that they never kiss. She chalks that up to him respecting her and being a "good Christian." After all, they met at church, right?

I'm not saying you can never be a genuinely platonic friend with a man. Karen and Jim, my dear friends and coauthors on my first two books, were just that for six years before their close friendship and business relationship turned romantic. The difference between them and Thomas and Maggie is that Karen and Jim *both* considered each other "pals" until God opened their eyes on the same day, and they realized they'd fallen in love. They've been blissfully married for more than twenty years. Thomas and Maggie, on the other hand, fit the typical scenario in which the man has no interest and is merely being polite, while the woman is falling in love by herself. Soon she's left with nothing but a broken heart.

What do you do if you find yourself in the same position as Maggie—falling in love with your buddy at church? Stop calling him, starting *today*. When you're around him, act the same way you always have. Just don't be the one to initiate the calls or get-togethers anymore. If the relationship is meant to be, he'll begin to miss you and start calling.

What if he confronts you and asks why you've stopped dialing his number? Act nonchalant and say something like, "I'm sorry. I've been so swamped! I sure miss talking to you, though. Give me a call; I'd love to catch up." That way you casually put the ball in his court without dramatically putting your heart on the line.

Tell Me About It!

To be honest, I never would have been able to avoid the "buddy syndrome," keep from advertising my feelings too soon, or handle the separation of long-distance romance if I hadn't had a strong support system. I was able to refrain from freaking out my dates while maintaining my sanity by daily doing three things:

1. I talked to God.

2. I talked to myself.

3. I talked to my girlfriends.

As we discussed in the secret on seeking divine intervention, I have made it a life habit to take every concern to God. He is the first person I run to throughout the day, whether I am driving (eyes open, of course), working, exercising, or cleaning house. I know he cares about the details of my life, so I never hesitate to talk to him about them.

I use my journal for two things—to talk to God and to talk to myself. Though I always begin each journal entry with "Dear Jesus," I'm really saying, "and Victorya too." During my single years, I regularly wrote my life sagas in my journal, either early in the morning or before I went to bed. I hope you have been developing that same habit by completing each secret's exercises in your own journal. I found that writing down my thoughts about my dates helped me tremendously. I could always go back later and psychoanalyze my situation. Sometimes just seeing the words on paper gave me a completely new perspective.

In addition to taking everything to God and writing in my journal daily, I had a solid group of girlfriends with whom I shared my love life on a consistent basis. Do *you* have a circle of support? Pull out your journal and list your current female friends from work, school, church, or your neighborhood. (It might help to go back to the cheerleader list you made in secret 4.) As you look over your list, ponder each friendship. Is it reciprocal or one-sided? Do you show genuine interest in your friend's life as well as talk about yours? Write down any ways you can think of to improve each friendship.

Now promise yourself you will not dismiss your girlfriends every time you start dating someone new. Cutting out girlfriends to spend all your time with a new man is one of the worst things you can do. You end up isolating yourself and missing the advantage of having people you can talk to about your relationship. You may very well miss "warning signs" about your guy that your friends would be able to see right away.

Rah-Rah Sisterhood

We all have needs, and that's OK. We're human. What's not OK is to burden a brand-new love (or any one person, for that matter) with the expectation that he will meet all of those needs. Ladies, it's in our female nature to overanalyze *everything*. Do your analysis with your girlfriends; don't freak out your new man. If your relationship is not moving forward according to your plans, stay calm. Complain to your girlfriends, not to him.

In my circle I had Cathy, Linda, Christine, Pam, Peri, Abby, Karen, Laura, my sister Teri, my sister-in-law Jennifer, and my mom (and that's not the exhaustive list!). Each of these ladies got phone calls or long talks over meals during the various man-related dramas in my life. I'm sure they were all thrilled that I had others in my circle; that way, none of them got stuck listening to me hour upon hour and day after day. I spread the misery! (When I think of all those hours I spent on the telephone with my girlfriends, it's hard to believe I actually had time to be a successful businesswoman.)

Maybe I'm at the extreme with my long list of supporters. It may not fit your personality to have a dozen girlfriends. Maybe you live in a small community where there just aren't a dozen girlfriends to be had. Or maybe you would never dream of wearing your heart on your sleeve, sobbing to the world around you. That's OK. I personally chose to build a large support team for my own sanity and to keep me from scaring dates away by being too needy. We all need cheerleaders and friends, be it one, five, or ten. I beg you to find at least one person, preferably three or more, with whom you can share your life. I promise, it will be good for you *and* for your man, whether he realizes it or not.

I do want to add one word of caution, however. Please use discretion when discussing your budding romance with your friends. You don't want to reveal your guy's personal confessions or spill other information he would consider private. That would be a breach of confidence. When he finds out (and he will), the trust you have worked so hard to build with him will be shattered.

IS IT TIME FOR THE D.O.R.?

Let's say you've been dating the new man in your life for a month, maybe three months now. You seem to be doing everything right. You're not freaking him out. You're depending on God, yourself, and your girlfriends to keep you sane. So when is it time to have the big talk? I'm referring to the D.O.R.—the good ol' "define our relationship" discussion.

D.O.R. is not about getting engaged. It's about finding out whether the two of you are in an exclusive relationship. If approached too soon, however, you might as well spell it D.O.O.R. Your guy will be out the door in an instant! So be careful. Don't let him think you're so insecure that you have to rush into a commitment (even if you feel that way). And don't stress early on about other women. Let him work up to choosing you above all others. It may take time for him to realize you're a prize worth winning.

So how do you know when you can safely risk the talk? The first month is almost always too soon to define a relationship as exclusive. But as months two, three, or four roll along, the D.O.R. may be appropriate. My best advice is to keep your eyes and ears open and pay attention to your man's signals.

Has he begun sharing his feelings with you, and does he seem open when you reciprocate? Is he seeing you consistently (at least once a week)? If not, he is either seeing other women, too, or he is too busy at work to commit to a relationship right now. Has he just broken off a relationship with someone else? If that's the case, he may be gun-shy or have unresolved issues with his past girlfriend. He will not be ready to commit his whole heart to you until he has worked through those feelings.

Of course, it's ideal if *he* brings up the subject; but if you really feel it's time and you just can't wait any longer, go ahead. Be bold and ask. You may *think* you're in an exclusive relationship; but until you discuss it, officially you're not.

A great excuse for bringing up the D.O.R. is if another man asks you out. Then you can go to your guy and say, "A friend of a friend just asked me to a concert, and I thought I should ask you first before responding. Do you consider us exclusive, or do you think we should be seeing others too?" You might add, "Where do you see our relationship going?"

Pay attention to his responses to your questions. Even if he's not ready to commit yet, his answers will give you valuable insight into when and if he's looking to be in an exclusive relationship. Then you can make your own choices accordingly.

It's not that men don't want to fall in love and get married. Most men do. But men want to ease into the whole concept. Commitment terrifies them. A wise man worth keeping wants to make the right decision at the right time. When a woman pushes for commitment too soon, his guard goes up, and the door of his heart slams shut. Obviously you don't want that. So don't freak him out! Don't rush him into exclusivity, fearing he'll stray elsewhere. Let him ease into it. Take it slow. Believe me, time *is* your friend.

Ultimately, your mission from date two until engagement is to keep your relationship progressing at a gradual, consistent pace, thereby inspiring your man to pursue you without getting bored. As long as you can keep him from feeling pressured, obligated, or outdone, like the frog in that lukewarm pot, he'll stick around—and maybe even fall head over heels in love.

KNOW YOUR *Limits*

Michael was the first guy who taught me that men pout. I was sixteen when we were reacquainted at a wedding after his family had spent several years overseas as missionaries. My, he had become quite the hunk! He was a senior and star football player at another high school, and he asked me out on my first car date. My parents let me go because they knew he was a good Christian boy.

Three dates later we were making out in his car when his hands wandered out of bounds. I stopped him with a thousand apologies. Michael drove me home in silence. I pleaded with him not to be angry with me, but he just kept driving, eyes forward, jaw tight. Finally he grumbled, "I'm not mad; I'm just disappointed." I didn't hear from him again. But those words and that pouting expression replayed in my mind for years.

I later learned that Michael was in a steady two-year relationship with a cheerleader at his school. I had been "the other woman." Me!

I couldn't believe it. I never had a chance! I'm so glad I stood firm.

Fifteen years later I was dating another athletic hunk. Sure enough, just like Michael in high school and countless men in-between, I saw the same pout and heard the same words: "I'm not mad; I'm just disappointed."

How far can you go on a first date, second date, all the way through engagement? The physical realm is an extremely difficult and emotional area for women to navigate. We *so* want to please. And sometimes we so desperately want our man to commit to marriage!

Will your guy fall deeper in love the further you go? Should you save yourself for that one special person?

Many women convince themselves they'll *just know* when Mr. Everything has appeared. *It will feel right*, they presume, and then giving in to temptation will be OK. Right?

Wrong.

Passion is just one of many factors in a good marriage, but it's the part that tends to get all the attention when people are choosing who to wed. Trust me. Your physical antenna will attract you to all sorts of men—including attractive creeps. So guard your heart and your body at all costs. You have only one body to give. Once you have given it away, you won't be able to give that precious gift again.

If you want to be a prize worth winning, it's critical that you take a firm position on how far you will go on a date. I'm not telling you to advertise your stance on the first date or even bring it up if you don't have to. But believe me, if you are dating a man, *any* man, sooner rather than later, the topic *will* arise.

It's up to you, ladies! Know your limits. I've heard this statistic over and over: a man supposedly thinks about sex every six seconds.

Oh my word! How monotonous! I mean, even if it's once an hour, the thought would wear thin, wouldn't it?

The fact is, men are wired differently than we are—on purpose. God designed men to be the rulers, the aggressors, and the protectors. He designed women to be the helpmates, the pursued, and the cherished. As a result, yes, men are preoccupied with sex; but the act alone is not what makes them commit to a relationship. Men can and do separate love and sex. Women don't. Women feel that sex equals love; men feel that *claiming* to be in love equals sex. There's a distinct difference between the two viewpoints.

John Gray, author of *Men Are from Mars, Women Are from Venus*, vividly describes the two sexes this way: "Men are like blowtorches and women are like ovens."[1] How true! Ladies, we are into romance, relationship, family, and the *idea* of love. Men are into sight, fantasy, challenge, and action. That's why men love watching sports, striving for success, and chasing women—it's all about competition and conquering.

Every man struggles with the temptation of sex, even a man worth keeping. Yes, there are wonderful Christian men out there with self-control. However, there are also many Christian men with good intentions but poor self-will. *Every* man has the potential to slip into premarital sex. It's up to you to set the boundaries and stand strong, whether he's proclaiming his undying love or expressing his grave disappointment.

GETTING PHYSICAL VERSUS GETTING PERSONAL

If you weaken and succumb to his pressure and charms, you're very likely to be blamed as his "temptress." You see, a man cannot live at peace with himself unless he is following his own internal code of ethics. When he veers off his moral path, he may put on a larger-than-life smile, but inside he feels guilt and unrest. The apostle Paul put words to this internal struggle when he wrote, "I do not understand what I do. For what I want to do I do not do, but what I hate I do" (Romans 7:15). If your man has been a Christian for long, I guarantee you, it's hard for him to be a happy sinner. God has ingrained those biblical values deep within his soul. As a result, if he sleeps with you—even if it was his idea—he may very well blame you for his downfall and eventually leave.

I know firsthand how confusing this can be, especially when the man comes on strong. Christian and non-Christian men come from the same mold when it comes to sex drive and motivation. John Gray clarifies the scenario well:

Certainly when a man is attentive to a woman, he could also be interested in having a relationship with her, but quite often he is not that discerning. To a certain extent, when he is enamored of a woman, he just likes what he sees, and he wants to touch. . . . What [the woman] doesn't know is that the next day he could be with someone who turns him on and feel the exact same feelings of attraction. Without this understanding of our differences, women assume that men are either deceptive or just superficial.[2]

It's not that all men are evil, deceptive, or shallow. They're just wired differently, and initially they pursue women based on physical attraction. Be bold enough to put on the brakes of passion. Give your guy a chance to move past mere attraction so he can get to know you inside and out. If you spend all your time making out (or more), you're not doing much to learn about each other, are you? Too often, getting physical replaces getting personal. Sex becomes a substitute for relationship.

Have you ever wondered how opposites attract? Odds are they're majoring in chemistry, not communication. And when the final grades come out, their relationship is likely to fail. Just look at all the broken marriages around you. What changed, when the two people used to be so madly in love? Maybe nothing. Perhaps they merely confused sex with love and woke up to find themselves married to strangers, with nothing in common but faded attraction.

The good news for "good girls" everywhere is that a man worth keeping may succumb to temptation and date a promiscuous woman for a while, but rarely will he choose to marry her. When he is looking for marriage, he will look for a woman who meets his ideal of virtue. Don't you want to be that one?

Red Light, Green Light

How far you go beyond kissing and embracing is a personal choice. What does your conscience say is far enough short of having sexual intercourse? Genesis 2:25 says that Adam and Eve, the first husband and wife, "were both naked and were not embarrassed or ashamed in each other's presence" (AMP). How far can *you* go without being naked, embarrassed, and ashamed? These are questions you need to answer *before* your first date. Keep in mind, your guy will assume that anything you do with him, you've already done with someone before him.

If and when a date pushes beyond your comfort zone, what should you do? Simply grab his hands and politely but firmly say no.

If he questions you, say, "It's too soon." If he pushes to know when it will be OK to go to the next level, tell him in a friendly, matter-of-fact tone, "I'm looking for a husband, and I know my husband would want me to save myself for him."

What if his next move is to look deeply into your eyes and say, "What if I'm that man?" Then you can reply in a soft laugh, "That would be wonderful! I'm sure you, especially, understand why I won't go further right now."

Pull out your journal and think of several responses you could give to a man who tries to go past your comfort zone. Write out a few scenarios and practice your responses out loud. You may feel silly, but isn't it better to have a plan than to be caught off guard and speechless?

Let's Go for a Test Drive

Frank and Kelly had spent the day at auto dealerships looking for cars. Later at his place, they both got carried away. Frank soared right past roadblocks previously heeded. When Kelly came to her senses and told him to stop, Frank blew out a disgusted sigh.

"Kelly, this is ridiculous," he said. "We've been dating for months. You know how I feel about you. Listen to me: If I gave you the keys to one of those cars we saw today, would you buy it without first taking it for a test drive? Heck, no! You'd want to see how well it runs first. That's all I'm trying to do for us, baby. It's time to see if we're meant for each other."

Please laugh out loud at any man who promotes the argument that you should "try out the merchandise before you decide to buy." You don't have to worry about being sexually compatible with your spouse if you forgo premarital sex. That's what kissing is for! If you feel passion together when you hold hands, kiss, cuddle, and coo, your chemistry will be there when you make love. If it's not "perfect" your first time, so what? You're married. You have your entire life to practice. Better to learn with someone you can trust!

If a man ever tells you (and some will) that he will not marry you until he knows the two of you are physically compatible, what he is really saying is, "I won't keep seeing you if you don't have sex with me." In other words, he is looking for casual sex. He is not looking for a wife. Run in the opposite direction! Your feelings may get hurt, but the pain won't be as bad as the heartbreak you'll suffer later if you sleep with him. Giving in to pressure to have sex *never* guarantees wedding vows. Even engagement doesn't guarantee that both of you will hang in there long enough to walk the aisle. Until you say, "I do," either of you can still say, "I don't." So don't slip up and give in until that much-anticipated, glorious wedding day!

Some single women decide to avoid temptation altogether and forgo all physical contact, even kissing, until they are in love, engaged, or even married. That's a personal choice. You must know your own limits. I do caution you, however, that if you don't eventually hold hands, embrace, and kiss at some point before the wedding, you won't know if you'll have chemistry together once you're married. You don't want to spend your life with someone with whom you share no feelings of real passion. That would be devastating to your self-esteem and his.

What if you've failed to set boundaries in the past and are far from a virgin? God can and will forgive you for any sin if you just ask him to. The Bible says in 1 John 1:9, "If we confess our sins, he is faithful and just and will forgive us our sins and purify us from all unrighteousness." If you are currently in a relationship with a man you're sleeping with, pray for God's wisdom and favor with your boyfriend as you tell him that you will no longer have sex outside of marriage. Tell him you've let yourself and God down by giving in to temptation. Say, "I hope that you love me enough to honor my new commitment. But if you have to leave, while it will break my heart, I will let you go." These are tough words; but if your man really loves you, he will stick around. If he doesn't, he was going to leave eventually anyway.

Here's another piece of important advice if you've overstepped your boundaries: don't give details about your past sexual experience (or ask for details about your guy's past relationships). Nothing good will come of it. Once you've shared that information, neither one of you will easily forget it, even if you get married. You don't want the image of you with another man forever etched in your husband's mind, do you? Take your indiscretions to God, ask for forgiveness, and forget about them from that moment forward.

If I could Turn Back Time

Take a few minutes now to go back to your journal, turn to a new page, and list all of your previous dating relationships. Then answer these questions:

1. How far did you go with each guy? (Use code language in case your journal falls into the wrong hands.)

2. How early into the relationship did you go that far?

3. What impact did it have on your relationship?

4. If you put up boundaries, what was his reaction?

5. How and why did the relationship end?

I'm not asking you to reminisce to cause you pain. I'm asking you to ponder your past so you can improve your future with your man worth keeping.

CREATED FOR PLEASURE

In John 10:10 Jesus says, "The thief [the devil] comes only to steal and kill and destroy; I have come that they may have life, and have it to the full." God is not a joy killer. He created sex to be a good thing—no, a great thing! God designed sex to be an incredibly wonderful, fulfilling activity, enjoyed between two life mates who have become one flesh legally, physically, and spiritually.

What God meant for good, however, Satan has perverted and corrupted. Don't be fooled by the lies plastered across magazine pages and movie screens. Casual sex does not bring happiness. True sexual fulfillment is found only in the marriage bed, the place for which it was designed.

Why does God forbid sex outside of marriage? Because once you've bonded with someone that way, you've given away a piece of yourself that you can't get back. Have you ever licked an envelope and sealed it, only to remember that you left something out? Did you notice that no matter how carefully you reopened the envelope, a jagged portion of the top part tore off and stuck to the bottom? That's what happens to us when we bond with another person through sex: a torn, jagged part of us is left behind.

No wonder the Bible says, "Flee from sexual immorality. All other sins a man commits are outside his body, but he who sins sexually sins against his own body" (1 Corinthians 6:18). *Flee* is the operative word here. It means to run in the opposite direction—not push yourself right up to the teetering edge of self-control and then hope you can stop. The fact is, the deeper and longer the kiss, the less will power you're going to have to stand your ground. And if *your* will power starts getting shaky, what do you think is happening to *his*? Even a polite gentleman can turn into a ravenous wolf when the door of passion is opened. Be aware and be wise!

God never intended to make our lives miserable with a tedious list of dos and don'ts. Every rule in his book, the Bible, was written to keep us from harm. One night of fun in the bedroom can lead to regrettable, life-altering results, from getting pregnant to contracting a sexually transmitted disease. If you and your guy both remain virgins until marriage, however, you'll never have to fear either consequence.

I like how the authors of *Love Tactics* put it: "Sure, premarital sex is highly prevalent in today's modern society. But look around you! Isn't unfulfilled love just as prevalent? You see, it's not that premarital sex is harmful because it's disapproved. Rather, it's disapproved because it's harmful! It spells the difference between a temporary relationship and a lasting one."[3]

Remember the old saying, "Why buy the cow when you can get the milk for free?" Your body is the ultimate gift you have to offer—a wonderful enticement for commitment and marriage. If you want to marry a man worth keeping, set your boundaries and don't waver.

Yes, chemistry is important. It's good to know it's there. But giving in to sex will do nothing to help build friendship, trust, and respect between you. And for your relationship to last, you will need all three.

So how far can you go without going all the way? It's your body and your future. Respect yourself enough to know your limits, set your boundaries, and stand firm. You deserve that—and so does your future husband.

FACE
Reality

When Heidi first met Jerry, he seemed larger than life. He was funny, confident, attentive, and lavished her with gifts. They took road trips, hung out with his friends, and spent time together almost 24/7, it seemed. About a month and a half into the relationship, however, things changed abruptly. They still hung out with his friends, and he still wanted to be with her all the time, but his sense of humor went from clean joking to poking fun. In fact, every time they were around Jerry's friends now, he entertained everyone by cruelly teasing Heidi. Embarrassed, Heidi would laugh along with the crowd; but later, when she was alone, she would cry.

It bothered Heidi that Jerry made her the butt of his jokes. It also bothered her that he seemed overly concerned about her every move. She felt guilty every time he asked her what she was doing when she wasn't with him. And then there were the Sunday-morning excuses. Sure, Jerry was a Christian; but each week, when Sunday rolled around, he said he couldn't make it to church because "things came up" or he was just too tired from partying the night before.

When I told Heidi these little "bothers" sounded like serious warning signs, she reasoned each one away. Jerry only poked fun at her, she said, when he drank too much. Yes, it was happening more frequently, but that was because he was under so much stress at work. Yes, she was having migraine headaches a lot lately, especially every time Jerry quizzed her about her whereabouts. But then, his ex-wife had cheated on him. He was trying to learn to trust again, and she needed to be patient.

"Why would you continue dating someone who leaves you crying more than laughing?" I asked.

"Victorya, you know how much I hate the dating scene," Heidi replied with a sigh. "It's just so nice to be 'off the market' and know that someone is there for me. And we had so much fun in the beginning. No one had ever treated me that well before. I just know that when Jerry's work situation calms down, things will get back to the way they used to be."

It makes me sad to see smart Christian women repeatedly make dumb choices in men. I want to shake them sometimes and shout, "Wake up! What are you thinking? At what point will you realize that a bad boyfriend makes a terrible husband?" It boggles my mind that a woman would consciously choose to ignore unacceptable, even abusive, behavior just to keep from being alone.

One of the things I've learned in life is that if it sounds too good to be true, it usually is. Beware. There is only one you. And you live in a world filled with impostors. There are plenty of charming, smooth-talking men ready, willing, and able to sweep you off your feet and use you for their own short-term pleasure. At all costs, guard your heart! As Jesus said in Matthew 7:6: "Do not give dogs what is sacred; do not throw your pearls to pigs. If you do, they may trample them under their feet, and then turn and tear you to pieces."

You've just spent eight chapters working on becoming an interesting and independent prize worth winning. Don't throw away all your hard work on a fool who will trample your progress to pieces!

I beg you: stay alert. And face reality. No matter how much you suffer from low self-esteem, don't assume that a guy is worth keeping just because he'll date you. Of course you want to be trusting. Of course you hope he's "the one." I'm not trying to turn you into a complete cynic. I'm not saying you should announce to every man, "Hey, you're cute and sweet, but I'm waiting for you to prove yourself before I feel anything for you."

I'm just asking you to realize that, like you, your guy is putting his best foot forward to try to win you over. That's flattering, of course; but with a little effort, anyone can put on an act for six weeks or even longer. Remember there's always more to a man than meets the eye, and you need to know what that "more" is before you commit your heart.

Have you ever been on cloud nine in a new relationship, absolutely certain you're dating the most amazing man on the planet, when suddenly—seemingly overnight—he changes? Where did your dreamboat go? The truth is, the curtain fell. The act is over, and the real person has emerged. Your boyfriend may offer a few spurts of his former self; but what you see now are his true colors, and they're here to stay.

So go ahead. Give your new guy the benefit of the doubt, hope he is genuine, and enjoy the ride. But keep your eyes wide open. Allow enough time to pass to determine if his reality matches his promise. Adopt a wait-and-see attitude. Be a woman worth winning who is optimistically cautious with her heart.

USING YOUR WOMAN'S INTUITION

Just because he's a "good Christian boy" doesn't mean he's a man worth keeping. Case in point: I was so excited to be pursued by Brian, the hottest bachelor at our church singles group. He was a devout Christian, popular, outgoing, athletic, and successful. Brian had lived in glamorous cities all over America. He was fun and creative at date planning. What more could a girl want?

But something wasn't quite right with this picture. You see, nothing kept Brian happy for long. Every two years or so, he took a transfer or promotion and moved to another town. He changed girl-friends more frequently than he changed jobs. Even though he was actively involved in church and Bible study, he was chronically rest-less and dissatisfied. Basically, he suffered from the grass-is-always-greener-on-the-other-side syndrome.

My woman's intuition warned me that Brian had a problem. I sensed that he had a wandering eye and was incapable of being faithful to one woman. And I was right. As painful as it was to face reality and follow my intuition, the second time Brian began to wander, I walked away for good.

It's been more than ten years; I've heard he's been engaged a time or two since. But he still always finds a reason to move on to the next girl. Clearly, something is missing in his life that he hasn't trusted God enough to uncover and deal with. I couldn't fix him; neither could countless other women, pastors, books, and Christian counselors. Brian has so much going for him—if not for that one fatal flaw. Until he chooses to let go of his grass-is-greener viewpoint and trust God to give him what's truly best, he will never be a man worth keeping.

Woman's intuition, a sixth sense, a gut feeling—whatever you call it, you know you've got it. It's that thing inside you that alerts you: *something is wrong with this picture.* When I was single, my warning was always a sick feeling in the pit of my stomach. I was sure I had ulcers every time it occurred. For you, it may be a pain in your neck, tension in your back, a severe headache, or a little voice whispering in your head. Somehow your body lets you know that trouble is on the horizon.

Pay attention to those signs! Don't rush for symptom relief— whether an aspirin or an antacid—without also stopping to look at what's going on in your relationship at that very moment. Right then, pull out your journal and write down what's on your mind. What's bothering you about your guy? It doesn't have to be something big; it may, in fact, seem very minor. Write it down anyway. Taking time to ponder what's bothering you now just might save you years of heartache down the road.

Of course, as you grow in your relationship, the man in your life will probably make a few mistakes. He will say something offensive, embarrass you in public, show up late, stand you up, or do something else that bothers you. As long as he isn't physically abusive (which merits no second chance), give him the benefit of the doubt. Realize he is human, and listen to his explanation. If it sounds feasible and reasonable, accept his apology. After all, miscommunication is a common occurrence in male-female relationships. Everyone has an off day now and then; we all get cranky or moody. Ladies, we're especially known for overreacting a day or two each month! So whenever there's conflict in your relationship, try to evaluate what's really happening. It may not be a big deal.

If a specific blunder happens a second or third time, however, you need to face the fact that you may be dealing with an unacceptable character flaw in your man. Decide if the behavior is something you are willing to live with. Try the objective approach: if *someone else* in your life were treating you this way, would you put up with it? If the answer is no, it's insanity for you not to end the relationship right then—no matter how much you think you like this person. As Benjamin Franklin is often quoted as saying, "The definition of insanity is doing the same thing over and over and expecting different results."

what you see is what you get

Ask yourself, *Am I being truthful with myself about my boyfriend? Or am I living in a dream world?* There are bad guys out there, including men who can put on a great "Christian act." But as author Beth Moore says, "God never called us to naiveté. He called us to integrity. There is a very big difference between the two. The biblical concept of integrity emphasizes mature innocence, not childlike ignorance."[1] Matthew 10:16 tells us we should "be wary and wise as serpents, and be innocent (harmless, guileless, and without falsity) as doves" (AMP).

So pay attention to what you see. Follow your gut. Don't ignore warning signs!

Let's pull out your journal again and take a few moments to face reality. Write down what you are getting from the man in your life right now. Describe him the way he is, not the way you want him to be. How is he treating you *right now*, not back in your first month of dating? Put down all of his good qualities—you know, the ones you keep bragging to your friends about. But also write out every complaint you've had.

Now ask yourself, what has your woman's intuition been telling you? Have you been getting headaches or stomach pains lately? If you were to say, "Something seems wrong with this picture," what would that something be? Write down whatever comes to mind.

Here's the real clincher: pull out your husband wish list and compare it to what you've just written about your current man. Are the two pages similar, or are they vastly different? What does that tell you about your relationship?

Beware the Angry Man

Tad was another handsome, outgoing, well-liked Christian guy I dated for a while. But again, I sensed there was something wrong with this picture. When we got together, his career and finances were a mess. He had a lot of residual pain from past relationships and a difficult childhood. He always seemed to hold out hope that great success was on the horizon, but his past failures haunted him and hampered his progress.

It took me awhile to realize that Tad was an angry man. I should have known by his constant criticism of my every move.

When others were around, he was always gracious, friendly, and funny; but when we were alone, he was often cruel. Back then I was in the midst of my people-pleasing years, and my self-esteem was low. So I ignored all the warning signs. After all, everyone liked Tad, and he chose me! *Wow, I must really matter*, I thought. But even that wasn't enough to lift my poor self-image. I also felt I had to *prove* my worth by attempting to fix Tad's problems.

It wasn't until our May-through-December relationship ended and I looked back over my journal that I realized our relationship hadn't been much fun. Tad's verbal abuse had escalated over the months. It hit a frightening peak one late afternoon while we were driving to a party. When he missed a turn, I politely asked, "Are you taking another route?" He stopped at the next intersection, reached over, grabbed me by the neck, and rocked my head back and forth. Then in a gentle, low voice, he said, "Oh, how you frustrate me. Hmm. I could break your neck right now, just like that, and you'd be dead." Then he smiled and asked, "Why do I tease you like that? Ha!" And he kept driving.

That was the first time Tad threatened me with physical harm. He didn't use an angry tone. But the threat was real. I was shaken and speechless.

I told my friend Pam what happened as soon as I got home that night. The next day, at six in the morning, she called me to say she had awakened from a terrible nightmare. She dreamed I had been murdered and was featured on the TV series *Hard Copy*. She begged me to break up with Tad right then. We prayed together. I cried, and a few hours later, I dialed Tad's number.

"I can't see you again until you go to a Christian counselor," I told him, hoping he cared enough for me to get help. The conversation seemed to hold promise, and Tad thought about the idea for a few days. But when he finally called back, his voice was filled with disdain. He said he didn't need counseling. He treated me "that way" because I drove him crazy.

"No one has ever caused me to act that way before, ever!" he claimed. Then he told me he had driven around all night praying about what he should do and that God told him to break up with me.

And you know what? I do believe God told him that. I was far too emotionally involved to end the relationship on my own. I needed a friend like Pam, who was brave enough to interfere and share her nightmare. And I needed Tad to do the official breaking up, so I wouldn't keep holding on. If only I had been strong enough to heed the words of Proverbs 22:24 early on: "Do not make friends with a hot-tempered man, do not associate with one easily angered." I would have saved myself a lot of pain.

I've been told Tad's life has turned around, and he is happily married with children. Tad had so much promise, but for that fatal flaw of a past not reconciled. Perhaps now it is. I hope so, for his family's sake.

Please be willing to face reality, no matter how painful the decision. If someone you are dating is wonderful to everyone else in the world but critical, rude, or mean to you, you must leave the relationship. Don't fall into the easy trap of thinking you're the problem and if you change, he'll treat you better. If he needs help, encourage him get it. But the two of you are not meant to be. He may be great around other people. But once he's established a pattern of disrespect toward you, his behavior will almost certainly continue.

HO, HO, HO or Bah Humbug!

For some people the Christmas holiday is a wonderful time of year to enjoy turkey, drink eggnog, and have fun catching up with relatives. For others it is an anxious time of walking on eggshells, tolerating personality clashes, and reliving painful memories. If you happen to be dating over Christmas, watch carefully to see which scenario best fits your guy.

Why does it matter? Because relationships with relatives, and especially with parents, have a significant impact on how a person responds to the opposite sex throughout all phases of life. So pay close attention to how your guy interacts with family members at Christmas (or any other time of the year). Watch how he treats his parents—especially his mom. How he views his mother has a lot to do with how he views women in general. If he cherishes his mother, he will cherish you. If he disrespects his mother, he will disrespect you.

Before you agree to marry this man, face reality head-on by making sure you spend quality time with his family. If that isn't possible for some reason, at least spend time talking with him about his family and listening to how he speaks about them. How is their relationship today? Is his mother or father controlling of him still? Be aware that they have been in his life longer than you have, and they will continue to be an influence, even if they are estranged from him.

I'm not saying they are more important to him than you are. There is a reason God tells couples to "leave and cleave" when they get married. Genesis 2:24 says, "Therefore a man shall leave his father and his mother and shall become united and cleave to his wife, and they shall become one flesh" (AMP). You need to be confident that your guy will make you the number one priority in his life (after God) once you're husband and wife. He must choose you over his mother from the moment you say, "I do." That doesn't mean he has to stop caring about his mother (or the rest of his family); it just means that he must elevate you to a higher position on his priority list.

Keep in mind, though, there *is* a list. If you marry this man, you will not be marrying just him; you will be marrying his family too. Yes, you will be his number one priority; but his family will continue to matter. And the truth is, your in-laws can be a great blessing in your life. I think it's interesting that of all my boyfriends, the first potential in-laws I bonded with were my husband's parents. I have been blessed with two really wonderful additions to my family by having Bob and Pat Rogers in my life!

SPEAK UP NOW OR FOREVER HOLD YOUR PEACE

Jacqui wanted children practically since the day she was born, but she never *really* discussed it with her fiancé, Frank. Anytime they'd see a baby, Jacqui would gush all over the infant. Frank would keep his distance. Whenever the subject came up, Frank said it would be a long time before he was ready to be a parent. Jacqui didn't worry about his hesitancy; she was certain he would change his mind after a few years of marriage.

Five years later, though, he still wasn't ready. And by their tenth year of marriage, Jacqui's biological clock was ticking loudly. When Frank still refused to be a father, their relationship fell apart. All that trouble and heartache could have been avoided so easily—if only Jacqui had been willing to risk rejection and talk honestly about one of the deepest longings of her heart before she said, "I do"!

When we discussed being a great date in secret 6, I encouraged you to spend most of your time on the first few dates talking about *him*. That way, he has a great time talking about his favorite subject, and you learn valuable information that can help you decide if he's a man worth keeping. But if, by the fourth date or so, you're not actively sharing your own personal tastes, interests, and desires with him, something is wrong with this picture. If he shuts down all attempts to talk about *you*, then you've probably found yourself a self-absorbed, pompous bore. Even if he claims to be madly in love with you, he doesn't really love you; he loves the fact that he has an attentive audience.

You deserve someone who's as interested in you as you are in him. As your relationship develops, make sure you're actively sharing your hopes, dreams, and goals for the future. How else will you know if the two of you are compatible? I mean, if he's planning on a hectic career in New York City and you see yourself as a missionary in Africa, one of you is in for a rude awakening!

NO Time to Pretend

Do you ever find yourself pretending to be whatever you think your man wants? For example, do you hate Chinese food yet find yourself frequently ordering hot-and-sour soup and Hunan beef, since it's his favorite meal? Even though you'd rather have a root canal than sit through one inning of a baseball game, does he think baseball is your favorite sport?

Stop that right now! If you try to change your personality to please a man, you'll be stuck being an imposter forever in order to keep him. There's a difference between being a good sport and trying new things versus claiming you love something you hate just to please someone else. Speak up! A man deserves to know the truth as much as you deserve to share it. We can all play roles for a while; but at the end of the day, we just want to be ourselves, don't we? If you stay authentic whenever you're with a man, you'll never have to wonder if he likes the real you. The real you will be the only you he knows.

Here's another topic to speak up about: money. If a man's finances are a disaster, that's usually a sign of irresponsibility, sloppy spending, or lack of self-control. You need to be sure you understand your guy's financial situation before you become engaged. If he handles money poorly when he's single, he'll handle it poorly when you're married. And money problems can be an overwhelming strain on even the best relationships.

Be courageous. Talk about the tough issues before you put on the ring. One of the worst things you can do is avoid difficult subjects or allow fear to keep you from telling the truth—whether the topic is where you want to live, how many children you want to have, or whether you want to keep your career after marriage or children. It's far better to discover potential incompatibilities while you're dating than to uncover them on the honeymoon. Save yourself thousands of dollars in marriage counseling by telling it like it is. Speak up now, or forever hold your peace!

Listen Up!

While you're speaking up, however, make sure you're listening too. John is a confirmed bachelor and proud of it. He says so to everyone he knows and every girl he dates. He loves his job, his money, his freedom, his boat, and his friends, and he doesn't want to change a thing. He is over forty, and even though countless women have suffered broken hearts attempting to change his mind, he remains a confirmed bachelor.

If you find yourself dating a man like John, cut your losses now. Let someone else be devastated when she finally realizes he's been telling the truth. If any man tells you something contrary to what you are looking for in a spouse, listen to him! If he says he doesn't want marriage, children, God, or the pressure of responsibility, believe him and walk away—politely, but quickly.

Face the possibility that you want this "bad boy" because you can't have him. Are you caught up in a cycle of chasing what you can't have? Are you in love with someone who doesn't love you back? Perhaps it's not really love; perhaps it's a longing to prove your self-worth by capturing someone who doesn't want to be caught.

It's common for a woman to fantasize that she'll be the *one* girl to reform a confirmed bachelor. Romantic movies are made all the time about the elusive "bad boy" who won't commit. We swoon and sigh as we watch him finally fall in love with the one woman who can change his mind, and we secretly dream that we are that woman. But we're not. We're simply caught up in fairy tales and movie rentals. The real world involves real people and real hearts. If a man tells you he's not interested in long-term commitment, marriage, or any other thing you hold as a virtue, you owe it to your-self to listen and believe him.

THE IMPORTANCE OF FRIENDS

My friend Kara fell hard and fast for Kyle. He was a great conversationalist, had a great job, and thought she was pretty and smart. Yes, Kyle had some messy relationships in his past. He confessed to his share of mistakes, including cheating on his first wife. But he had met God and turned his life around. Kara couldn't believe she was lucky enough to find him. They enjoyed each other's company so much that Kara seldom had time for friends and family anymore.

Six months later Kyle was in crisis. He received notice that his ex-wife was suing him for back child support, withholding visitation rights, and threatening jail time. Kyle was beside himself and clung to Kara for emotional support. Of course he wanted to pay child support, he told her, but his home, car, and business expenses were so high, it was impossible to keep up with all the payments.

Concerned that I hadn't seen Kara in a long time, I finally pinned her down for lunch. When I pressed her to fill me in on her relationship with Kyle, she did so with great reluctance. And as I'm sure she expected, I flatly told her that I didn't think God's best for her was a divorced businessman who wouldn't pay his child support!

"What you see is what you get," I said. "And how he treats someone in the past is a good indication of how he will treat you in the future—from cheating to neglectful parenting."

"Kyle has changed," Kara snapped back. "Can't he be forgiven? Should God punish him forever and not let him find love again?"

"Of course someone can choose to change," I responded. "Sure,

God forgives and allows us to love again. But, Kara, if you want to marry a man worth keeping, at least date someone who is caught up on his child support!"

Two years later Kara finally faced reality and walked away. It turned out that because she would not sleep with him, he had been finding fulfillment elsewhere. Kara was heartbroken, but at least she accepted the truth before she walked down the aisle to an eventual divorce.

If you find yourself deliberately avoiding family and friends when you begin seeing someone new, you know deep inside that you're dating the wrong person. Value counsel from trusted loved ones as a priceless commodity. Seek their wisdom. Ask your friends and family for advice. They can see things you can't. Sure, maybe one of them has ulterior motives—you know which friend or relative that could be. I'm not saying you have to agree with everything they say. I'm just saying it's wise to seek objective feedback from people you trust.

When you discuss your man, chances are you'll share complaints that you will foolishly ignore later, when you're more emotionally invested in the relationship. Hopefully your loved ones will remember and remind you of those red flags. Keep an open mind, and carefully evaluate whatever your friends and family are saying. If every person in your life is warning you about a particular man, wake up and wise up!

MISSIONARY DATING: TO DO OR NOT TO DO

I had a passionate debate with one of my best friends today. We were discussing whether it's ever OK for a Christian to "missionary date" (that is, date a non-Christian). We're both addicts of the TV reality show *The Bachelorette*, and we were discussing the previous night's episode, when a particular bachelor was dismissed from being one of the last three contestants. The reason? His mother made it quite clear that he was a Christian who would always put God first, wife second, and children third.

"Oh, the mother was so overbearing," Kelly told me. "She should have waited until the relationship was more solid to be so direct with his girlfriend."

My take? I thought the mom was right on. Everything she said was true. She spoke her heart. Yes, for a person who is not a committed believer in Jesus Christ, those would be overpowering words to hear. Sure, they could easily scare away a potential mate. And maybe the mom could have said what she said in a less confrontational way. But the message was apparently honest and accurate, because the bachelor didn't deny or make excuses for his mom's statements. Perhaps he was relieved that she said what he'd been holding back.

When should the topic of faith come up in a relationship? When should you let a date know that your faith in Jesus Christ is the central focus of your life? And when should you ask him about his faith? On the first date, ladies! Your relationship with Jesus should not be kept secret. It's a vital part of who you are. How can you hide it? Why would you want to?

As for inquiring about your date's relationship with God, or lack thereof, here's a tip for getting the information in a nonthreatening way: simply ask him about his spiritual upbringing. Did he go to church as a child? If so, what did he think about it? If he didn't go to church, what is his view of God? Be bold enough to ask those questions. Just be gracious, too, and genuinely interested in hearing his answers about his personal spiritual journey.

I urge you to commit yourself right now to marrying a man who shares your faith. Don't compromise, no matter how long it takes to find the right guy. The Bible says, "Do not be yoked together with unbelievers. For what do righteousness and wickedness have in common? Or what fellowship can light have with darkness?" (2 Corinthians 6:14). You may have strong feelings for a man who doesn't know God, but what could you possibly have in common besides physical attraction to support your relationship in the long run?

What if the guy is open to your faith and seems to have a lot of potential for becoming a Christian? Can you date him then? I did exactly that and got hurt. Oh, I figured it was OK, since there were several Christians in this man's life and he seemed interested in reading the Bible I gave him. But in the end, he was not seeking God; he was pursuing me.

Don't get emotionally involved with a man unless or until he becomes a Christian. You'll be putting too much at risk—your marriage, your children, and potential generations to follow. If you find out your date is not a Christian, choose to be platonic friends. Invite him to church or group activities. Introduce him to some hip Christian guys and pray that they hit it off and become buddies. But don't continue pursuing romance.

"But," you may argue, "Jesus didn't avoid sinners. He was actively involved with non-Christians and shared the gospel message with them. So why can't I date unbelievers as a way of winning them to Jesus?"

Despite a popular novel to the contrary, Jesus did not date. He was never romantically involved with anyone. That is a very important distinction. Go ahead and share Jesus with your guy friends. But don't "missionary date." You risk becoming more deeply involved than you ever intended—and more likely to go past the boundaries you set for yourself.

I know of only three examples of Christians who dated unbelievers and won them to Jesus. But I can tell you dozens upon dozens of stories of relationships that started the same way and ended in disaster. The three successes involved devout Christians who made their faith an open and conspicuous part of the dating relationship from the very beginning. They talked about God every time they were with their dates. They brought them to church every Sunday. They made it clear that the only way they would keep going out was if their dates genuinely sought a relationship with Jesus.

Maybe you're concerned that your "selection pool" will be significantly reduced the minute you decide to date only believers. You're absolutely right. But then, you only need to find *one* man worth keeping.

God wants the best for you, and so do I. I'm not here to judge you. I'm here to remind you that, practically speaking, you will only marry from the pool of men you date. So why tempt fate by getting emotionally involved with someone with whom you are "unequally yoked"?

Yes, I know, Christians are far from perfect. My most painful breakups were with Christian men, because I expected so much from them. Just because a guy loves Jesus doesn't make him a man worth keeping. But think about the future for a moment. If your spouse is not a believer, how will you relate during difficult times? I can assure you, there will be plenty of trying times in your marriage, whether they involve your career, children, health, finances, or some other crisis. The two of you will need strength from God to survive.

That's why my prayer for you is that you will commit to the one major criteria I held out for: someone who is your spiritual equal. Marriage is wonderful—I desperately love my husband!—but we're human, and we have conflicts at times. I honestly don't know how we would have made it this far if we weren't spiritually grounded. I am blessed every day to see Will make Bible study and prayer a priority in his life. When conflict does occur, we both respond first with prayer. Isn't that what you want too?

My dear friends Jim and Karen Covell believe the key to their successful marriage is the fact that they pray together ever single day—and have done so for more than twenty years. Don't settle! A man who will make prayer a centerpiece of your life together is a man worth waiting for.

THE GOOD, THE BAD, AND THE UGLY

Do any of the true stories I've shared thus far seem extreme, maybe even ludicrous? As I've read the stories back to the friends who lived them, many have responded, "Oh my, am I really that pathetic?" Sometimes it takes seeing your life written down in the third person to make you face reality!

Want to test that theory? Turn to the next blank page in your journal and take a few moments to write the story of your present or past relationship in the third person. Use fictitious first names for you and the guy involved, but keep all the details true. Then have someone else read the story out loud to you. Does it sound ridiculous? Is the lead male character a man worth keeping, or is he a man the woman in the story should run from as fast as she can?

Relationships shouldn't be complicated. Boy meets girl, boy likes girl, boy spends exclusive time with girl, boy wants to marry girl. Keep it simple! I used to be one of those women who bored my friends with lengthy justifications of why I should stay with a guy who clearly wasn't right for me. Don't make the same mistake. Cut to the chase, skip the long saga, and face reality. Is he available, honest, trustworthy, responsible, kind, fun to be with, and dedicated to God? If not, you are in for self-inflicted pain and suffering.

Pay attention to what you're really getting from your man. Don't get caught up in his "potential." What you see is what you get. In your journal, document the good, the bad, and the ugly. Go back over your own words whenever your emotions are getting the best of you. Finding a man worth keeping is all about sacrificing short-term pleasure for long-term happiness.

Throughout my dating life, I prayed the following prayer. I encourage you to pray it too:

Dear Jesus, help me in my relationship with [insert your boyfriend's name] today. If he is your will for me, keep us growing closer until we're ready for marriage. If he is not your will for me, make it clear to me and give me the courage to walk away. If I am too weak to do so, then I ask you to cause him to break up with me. Though I would be devastated, I trust you have my best interests at heart and will bring the right man into my life in due season. Amen.

God always answered me when I prayed those words. Sometimes he answered by showing me that a certain man wasn't for me, and I ended the relationship. Many times he answered by having the guy break up with me, because I was too weak to follow through. But the end result was the same—a man worth losing was gone, and I was available for the man God had for me all along.

So take courage from my example. Don't compromise. Stay committed to finding a man who is truly worth keeping. At every stage of a new relationship, be willing to walk away if the promise and the reality don't match. And trust God. If his plan for you includes marriage, you can be sure he's working right now to bring the right man into your life.

CALL IT LOVE OR *Call It Quits*

Will and I had been dating a few months when we both felt, "This is it." We talked briefly of marriage, going so far as to casually discuss the month we might tie the knot the following year. We were not officially engaged. It was too soon; we had been dating less than six months at that point. Still, I so wanted to believe Will was all I hoped him to be! Even with all my baggage from past disappointments and two previous failed engagements, I was eager to move forward.

Oh, the pressure! Poor Will. This was the first time he had been ready to get married. He was looking forward to shopping for rings together. I deprived him of that experience—I told him I'd been there, done that, and those relationships had fallen apart. Of course, what happened in the past wasn't his fault. In hindsight, I'm sorry I wasn't willing to budge on the matter. I was being illogical and ridiculous.

We were at odds on one other thing too. Will wanted his proposal to be unanticipated, memorable, and in his timing. I wanted it to happen, like, *yesterday*. The nonverbal pressure mounted for months. We were desperately in love, but the tension was nearing a breaking point. Every time we were together, I wondered, *Is he going to pop the question today?* If we drove to a romantic spot or went out to eat at a nice restaurant, I'd think, *Maybe this is the place he's going to ask for my hand.*

I so anticipated the question that I couldn't relax and simply enjoy dating. At least I knew better than to continually ask, "When are you going to propose?" But each time he boarded a plane for Oklahoma leaving my third finger still bare, my disappointment was poorly hidden.

One evening we were standing on the top floor of a parking structure overlooking the Santa Monica pier, staring at a beautiful sunset falling over the Pacific Ocean. The setting was magnificent and romantic—but Will was silent. *Another weekend is slipping away without a ring*, I thought. Will could sense my disappointment, and he wasn't happy about it either. He was not going to be forced to get engaged.

"What are you going to do if I don't propose for another few months?" he finally asked.

"I don't know," I said in a near whisper.

He expected that I was going to demand he propose or leave. But I wasn't ready to give that ultimatum. I wanted him. I was just sad and afraid we would never actually make the leap. So, he flew home, neither of us knowing what the future held.

Midweek he called and said he'd found an airfare special for the weekend. "I'd like to come out and see you, but only if you under-stand I will not be proposing while I'm there," he said. Quite frankly, I was relieved. Of course I wanted to see him. And I was ex-hausted from wondering if every turn in the car was taking us to an engagement destination.

That was the weekend he proposed. He had been waiting for the ring to arrive. He pulled off the proposal he wanted—unanticipated, memorable, and in his own timing. He proposed right before taking me to an Angels' baseball game in Anaheim. I never enjoyed a sporting event so much in my life. And I don't even recall who won! I just remember weeping over the national anthem—not because of the song (which I dearly love), but be-cause I kept thinking about the ring on my finger and the man at my side. *This is real. He chose me!* I was finally getting married to my man worth keeping.

DO YOU TRULY LOVE THIS MAN?

What about the man you're seeing? Will it be happily ever after and wedded bliss, or good-bye yellow brick road and buckets of tears? Time will tell. But if you find yourself obsessing about a ring and wondering if you should give him an ultimatum, make sure you have already answered a few critical questions:

1. Do you truly love this man? Or are you merely addicted to each other and you're mistaking that addiction for genuine love?

2. Are you fixated on the chase of an elusive bachelor and mis-interpreting your feelings?

3. Have you fallen for an image, or do you love the real person you've discovered behind the façade?

4. Is God the center of your relationship? Is he *any* part of it?

You owe it to yourself and to your guy to search for these answers. Before you start picking out china patterns and bridesmaids' dresses, you need to be sure your husband wish list and your boyfriend are one and the same.

Pull out the latest version of your wish list right now, including all the modifications you've made as you've discovered who you are and what you really want in a man. Rewrite the list, substituting your guy's name everywhere you previously wrote "my husband." Now read your final draft out loud. Do you recognize this person? Is he an accurate description of the man you've found?

If you come to a sentence or paragraph that does not honestly describe your guy, determine if the issue is a core value or a minor perk. For example, if you want to marry a man who attends church and your boyfriend doesn't, you're dealing with a core value. If you'd like a man who throws frequent barbecues and your guy hates to grill out, you're probably dealing with a minor perk. Be brutally honest as you consider the depth of your love and compatibility with this person. After all, your whole future is at stake!

THE ULTIMATUM D.O.R.

Do you feel you've reached the point where you must either call it love and commit to marriage or call it quits and cut your losses? When you date anyone for an extended length of time, periodic "define our relationship" talks are a natural part of the process. That doesn't mean asking, "When will you propose?" every other date. No, I promise that won't go over well! But you have every right to ask and to know where your relationship is headed.

Some women assume that men hold all the power when it comes to popping the question. If that's true, proposing must be easy for them, right? Wrong! Believe it or not, men get quite anxious about the engagement, even when they're sure they'll get an affirmative answer. I was surprised at how nervous my husband was when he proposed, especially since everyone in America knew I'd say yes!

When I asked Will later why he had acted so strangely, he told me it wasn't because he was worried about my answer; rather, it was because he realized the enormity of the sacrifice he was making. He was losing the freedom of living on his own from that day forward. Men do not give up their freedom lightly! Yes, he loved me and wanted to spend the rest of his life with me; but he was also fully aware that marriage meant maturity, responsibility, and accountability. No more carefree bachelorhood!

You see, ladies, we may have careers; but at the end of the day, we usually have a choice about whether we want to continue working in the marketplace or stay home and be a mom and homemaker. The man doesn't have that same choice. He is forever expected to be his family's provider, protector, and spiritual leader. Perhaps understanding the man's point of view will help ease any irritability you feel about *your* guy's reluctance.

Every man handles the release of his freedom differently. Some are ready to take the leap, and they jump on their own; some tiptoe to the edge of engagement, waiting for a sign that jumping is OK;

others just need to be conspicuously pushed. I don't know which kind of man you're dating. But when you've been together for quite a while and you're ready to move to the next level, it's completely fair for you to find out.

So how do you approach the ultimatum D.O.R.? Plan a time to honestly share with your guy how you feel. Pick an appropriate time to chat—definitely not when you're moody or when he's overwhelmed with work. Think through what you'll say ahead of time. Your journal and your girlfriends can help. Write out and practice your speech. If your words are overbearing, hopefully reading them out loud or getting feedback from your friends will fix that. Remember, you're not scolding him for not proposing; you're simply asking him where he thinks the relationship is going. Is he planning to marry you, or is he unsure of the future?

winter, spring, summer, or fall

How long should you date before taking the next step of getting engaged? It depends. The appropriate length of a courtship varies with the maturity and age of both partners. A safe dating guideline for any age group is two years. If you're a teen or a college student, I recommend two years as a *minimum* since the school years are a time when you're still "finding yourself." So much change takes place, especially when you're fresh out of high school—the "age of metamorphosis," I call it. You're developing your career aspirations, your dreams, and your life purpose. You need to allow plenty of time to find out if you and your guy are really on the same journey.

If you're out of school, in your thirties, forties, or beyond, I recommend a minimum of one year before taking the leap from "I may" to "I do." Seeing someone through all four seasons is enlightening. People behave differently throughout the year as they experience holidays, vacations, and the highs and lows of daily life. How does your guy respond to deadlines and work pressures, illness and fear, money and economics, politics and news headlines, holidays and relatives? You need to give yourself enough time to find out. A person's true character shines during life's two extremes: extreme success and extreme stress. Have you known your man long enough to watch him experience one or both?

You'd think nothing in Hollywood would surprise me anymore, but it never ceases to amaze me how drastically some people change when they go from years of struggling to "sudden" fame and fortune. Some stay the same genuine persons they always were. Others turn into arrogant jerks who spout off things like, "Don't you know who I am?"

Well yes, I do, I'm thinking. *But apparently you forgot!*

Here are my questions to you: have you been with your man long enough, and do you know him well enough, that you will recognize him during the good times and the bad times of your future life together? Or will a sudden change in circumstances, for better or for worse, change him into someone you've never met? Because I guarantee you, after marriage, you will have both triumph and tragedy. That's life. God never promised us a thorn-free rose garden (although he did promise us a Gardener who will never leave us nor forsake us!).[1]

Is your man maturing in his faith a little bit every day? Does he habitually allow God to carry him through the storms of life? Or does he withdraw when trouble arises and attempt to handle life on his own? The only way you'll know is by experiencing life together over a period of time. That's why I say that one year of exclusive dating is good; two years is better.

If you want to date longer than two years, go ahead. Just keep in mind that if you want to start a family someday, you don't have the luxury of auditioning a man indefinitely. The reality is, the biological clock *is* ticking, and you can't afford to waste half a decade or more on a man who cannot or will not commit.

Quite frankly, some relationships get stuck in limbo—one person is comfortable dating indefinitely, while the other is anxiously awaiting an imminent proposal. If you've been dating the same guy for many years, you need to face the fact that *one* of you is not interested in marriage and perhaps never will be. Two years is plenty of time for two mature people to know if they love each other enough to take the leap.

Two Ways to Leave Your Lover

Let's say you've been together a year or more. You've answered the tough questions and determined that you truly love your man. You've prepared the ultimatum D.O.R. and are ready to risk it all by asking for the assurance that you will be *married* within the year (or eighteen months, or two years—only you will know what's right for your situation). You are ready to let him know that he is free to propose whenever he'd like, as long as he respects the fact that you'll need time to plan a wedding. You just want to know you're on the same path.

Don't take this D.O.R. talk lightly. You have to mean what you say and be willing to act on whatever response you receive. Quite possibly he'll say, "I'm not ready to take the next step, and I'm not sure I ever will be." At that point, you must love yourself enough to walk away. The fact is, sometimes you have to break up to make up. He may come back, and he may not. If he doesn't return, then he wasn't going to marry you anyway, and you would have wasted more prime single years on a lost cause.

Here's the kicker, though: if you don't get the answer you were hoping for, you must be gracious. You don't know what the future holds; if he's running scared, a gracious response leaves the door open for him to change his mind and think, *Maybe I made a mistake. Maybe she is the one.* That's what you want! If you make a scene and respond with anger and bitterness, however, you slam that door shut. He'll simply be relieved to be free and keep on running.

If you are gracious and hold out hope for reconciliation, you have two options. The first is to cut all ties. The second is to allow him to continue dating you while you begin to date other men. Of course, that means he's free to date other women too. If you don't think your emotions can handle dating him while both of you are free to go out with others (that was my fragile state during breakups), choose total separation. If he loves you and just hasn't realized it yet, he needs time away from you to see what he's missing. Make it perfectly clear that he is not to call you—not even just to chat—if his feelings have not changed. (Commit to yourself that you will not call him either!) You need to be free to mourn the loss and move on with your life. If you allow him to call you, each time you hang up the phone, you'll feel as if you're losing him all over again.

If you think you can handle seeing him, knowing that a permanent breakup is still possible, then choose the second option, and force yourself to begin casually dating other men. Pull out your cheerleader list from secret 4 and jump back into circulation. He will miss you, but it will take him time to realize why. Is his pain a symptom of withdrawal from his addiction to you? Or does he really love you, and he can't live without you?

No Pain, No Gain

After my guy dumped me for the latest blonde visiting our church, I was so mad that I marched right out to the hair stylist that very day and cut twelve inches off my long blonde hair. I just *knew* that would punish my old boyfriend, since he always raved about how much he loved my locks. What was I thinking? Can you say "dumb blonde moment"? Little did it occur to me as I sat in that salon chair that I wouldn't be punishing my old flame. (Hello? He dumped *me*, remember?) I was punishing myself. It took me two years to grow my hair back.

Breaking up is heart-wrenching, whether the separation is permanent or temporary. You do illogical things, such as changing hairstyles, churches, cars, even jobs. You embarrass yourself in public while making a scene in front of your ex-boyfriend. You cry until your emotions are numb. You look at food and either gorge yourself or starve. Suddenly the idea of sleeping for the next five years sounds appealing.

If and when this happens to you, you need to remind yourself: *I am a prize worth winning.* That means you are a woman who is willing to feel your pain, because you know you have something to gain from it. As Romans 8:28 promises, God has a plan for your life, and somehow he'll bring something good out of your current crisis. Believe it!

The day of your breakup, pull out your calendar and mark off the next twelve weeks. Why twelve weeks? As we've said before, anyone can play a role for about six weeks; then the real person emerges. Six weeks of being without you may be sufficient time for your ex to discover whether he loves you or not. Double that length, and he's surely had enough time to discover his true feelings. If he doesn't come back to you by then, chances are he is gone for good. Watch your calendar and move on.

I've been through my share of twelve-week, wait-and-see periods. Sometimes the man came back, sometimes he didn't. By having a designated mourning period, I gave myself the OK to hold out hope without stranding myself in an indefinite emotional limbo.

As you count down the weeks, expect to face a full range of emotions—from hurt to anger to grief to relief. Spend some time alone, but also be careful not to isolate yourself. Talk with God. Hang out with your friends. Get involved in singles-group activities again. Begin a new hobby. Perhaps go on a few blind dates, and try to enjoy them. Move on with your life, even if you feel like a zombie going through the motions.

If your man comes back—even if it's long after the twelve weeks—you will have grown and maybe even changed. If you are available and still in love with him, hooray! Say yes, take the leap, and send out the invitations. He's your man worth keeping. If you're no longer available or your feelings have changed, celebrate that too. He was not your man worth keeping. Be glad you found out before it was too late!

Whatever you do, don't plunge into another serious relationship within the first three to six months after a split. You need time to contemplate, weep, and grieve. It's part of the healing process. Keep your head about you by writing ferociously in your journal, analyzing each new feeling as it comes. And find out if your ex really was "all that" by writing a brief history of your time together. Answer the following questions:

1. Was anything important missing from your relationship?

2. What could you have done better?

3. Were there any desires on your husband wish list that you ignored in order to stay together?

One of the most healing ways I found to purge myself of an old flame was to write a long good-bye letter—not one that I actually mailed, just a letter written *as if* he were going to receive it. In the letter, I would get out all my anger and hurt and ask all the questions I had in my heart. I wouldn't hold anything back. Then I would put it in a safe place so I could add to it later. In time I would shred the letter as a sign of closure. If you're relationship has come to a permanent end, you might want to try the same thing. Just make sure you hide the stamps!

EXTRA-STRENGTH PAIN RELIEF

A surefire path to rapid pain relief is to know ahead of time where to turn in a crisis. Only God can heal the broken pieces of your heart. He knows exactly what's going on with you, and he's ready, willing, and able to meet your need.

If there was ever a portion of Scripture to memorize for such a time, it's Romans 8:18–39. In this passage Paul reminds us who we are and on whom we can depend. He says, in part, "I consider that our present sufferings are not worth comparing with the glory that will be revealed in us. . . . No, in all these things we are more than conquerors through him who loved us. For I am convinced that neither death nor life, . . . neither the present nor the future, . . . will be able to separate us from the love of God that is in Christ Jesus our Lord."

There are other great places in the Bible to turn to after a breakup. Sometimes in my fragile state of suffering, I was in the mood to wallow in my misery by reading about the futility of life without God at the center—the Old Testament book of Ecclesiastes is a good one for that. Proverbs is *the* book for wisdom, understanding, and practical advice. Psalms is the perfect book of prayers. Every day, no matter what you're going through, *somewhere* in the book of Psalms you are bound to find words of prayer that are relevant to your situation. And no quick-reference guide for surviving pain and suffering would be complete without recommending the New Testament books of Philippians and James.

Wherever you choose to go in the Bible to lift your spirits and soothe your wounded soul, allow God to refine you in the fire of your current crisis. As you face the unknown future, pray with confidence the words of King David: "Be merciful and gracious to me, O God, be merciful and gracious to me, for my soul takes refuge and finds shelter and confidence in You; yes, in the shadow of Your wings will I take refuge and be confident until calamities and destructive storms are passed. I will cry to God

Most High, Who performs on my behalf and rewards me [Who brings to pass His purposes for me and surely completes them]! (Psalm 57:1–3 AMP).

Maybe your ex will discover that you are the one for him after all and rush back to propose. But even if he doesn't, you can be confident that God has a plan for your life—and if that plan includes marriage, it also includes who your spouse will be. Isn't it better to remain single and keep hoping for Mr. Right than to marry Mr. Wrong and be stuck in misery?

Forgive and Forget

A few years ago, I watched a TV interview of a woman who was serving a life sentence in prison. Ten years earlier, she had caught her millionaire husband in bed with another woman and reacted by brutally murdering both her husband and his mistress. As I listened to this woman spew venom on her deceased husband's memory, it was apparent to me that she was not only locked up in a literal prison but she was also confined in her own private prison of anger, bitterness, and consuming hatred. Killing her husband was not enough to release her from the power she allowed him to wield over her—both in life and after his death.

How vivid a picture her story paints of the need we all have to forgive those who hurt us! Revenge *never* releases us. It just perpetuates our own misery.

You will probably date a number of men before you find the one who's a "keeper." That means there's a good chance you will get hurt at some point in your dating life. The question is, will you respond with anger and bitterness, or will you forgive? Boy, I know how hard it is to let things go. But life is too short to hold long-term grudges against old flames.

Do everything in your power to forgive. Your mental health depends on it. So does your physical health. In fact, according to a recent study, "chronic unforgiveness causes stress. Every time people think of their transgressor, their body responds. Blood pressure and heart rates go up. Facial muscles tense, stress hormones kick in." Chronic stress, in turn, affects the immune and cardiovascular systems. But forgiveness reduces stress by replacing "negative emotions with positive ones."[2]

Why should you forgive your ex when he may not appreciate it or even know about it? Because you're not forgiving him for his sake; you're forgiving him for your sake—so you can reduce your stress, move on, and live life again. Why allow someone who hurt you the privilege of continuing to affect your life when you're better off without him anyway? When you choose to let him off the hook emotionally, you release the "death grip" he's had on you. Finally, you can live again!

Understand, forgiveness doesn't mean removing the consequences of wrongdoing. I believe in justice; and if you do the crime, you do the time. But God and government are responsible for vengeance and sentencing, not you and me. Forgiving a guy doesn't mean you're saying that what he did was OK, not by any stretch of the imagination. It doesn't mean you have to keep him in your life or continue a relationship at some level. Rather, forgiving him means you're choosing to no longer put your time and energy into the hurt he's caused. You are willfully turning your pain over to God and letting go.

I had an especially difficult time forgiving one ex-boyfriend. I was in seminary at the time, and I knew God wanted me to forgive the guy. He had been so cruel to me that no matter how earnestly I said the words, "I forgive," the pain still burned in my heart. It took me two years to fully let go. Then one day when I was in an office supply store, of all places, this man came to mind—and I didn't feel any pain. God revealed to me that hurt people hurt people. All the cruel words this guy had ever uttered had come from a wounded heart. I now pitied him rather than resented him. I was finally free!

STARTING OVER AGAIN—AND AGAIN

On one bone-chilling, snowy day, I approached the customs officer at the international terminal. Moments before, I had said good-bye for good to fiancé number two. Our love hadn't been strong enough to overcome our differences. The reality was, we had different values, different priorities, and different dreams, and it was time to cut our losses. I felt no anger—just overwhelming sadness. My eyes were all but swollen shut as I handed the officer my passport. After silently inspecting my papers, that precious man looked up at me and said something I will never forget: "You know, honey, for every deep sorrow in life, there will be an equal or greater joy to come later. Life just seems to balance itself out that way."

What salve to my wounded soul! His words of wisdom echoed those of Solomon in Ecclesiastes 3:1–4: There is a time for everything, and a season for every activity under heaven: . . . a time to weep and a time to laugh, a time to mourn and a time to dance." You may be sad today, but your day of joy will come! Things always work out for the best when God is involved.

The fact is, if I hadn't broken up with my various boyfriends (or if they hadn't dumped me when I wasn't strong enough to do the right thing), I wouldn't have been available when my husband came along. *Thank you, Jesus, for staying involved in my dating life!* Proverbs 16:9 says, "In his heart a man plans his course, but the LORD determines his steps." Isn't it encouraging to know that you can make your plans, but God will ultimately direct each step you take? He has your best interests at heart, and he alone knows how to get you where you really want and need to be.

So whether you've lost at love once, twice, or a hundred times, don't throw in the towel just yet. Don't settle for the next Mr. Good Enough. Promise yourself you'll stay committed to finding a man who is truly worth keeping. Remember, nothing is impossible with God.[3]

CALL IT LOVE

When you do finally find Mr. Right—the one you've prayed for, the one who matches most (if not quite all) of your husband wish list, the one you truly love and who truly loves you in return—then sit back, relax, and enjoy. Even if you are as overeager for that ring as I was, use every ounce of restraint you can muster to allow your man to spring his marriage proposal on you in his own perfect timing. Let him have that pleasure!

I admit I was ready for weeks, even months, before I finally heard the words, "Will you marry me?" But in hindsight, I realize Will really didn't keep me waiting that long. What are a few months compared to fifty years together as husband and wife?

Give yourself permission to simply enjoy this dating phase with the man of your dreams. Enjoy the fact that you can both say, "I love you" freely now without fear of scaring each other away. Enjoy the courtship, the flowers, the dinners, the planning for the future. Enjoy the long, precious hours of talking to one another on the phone and in person. Those talk fests are unique to this stage of love! During our latter dating months, Will and I talked on the phone for hour upon hour, often long past midnight. Today we laugh and wonder what we could possibly have had to say to each other to cover so much time. But back then, unending conversation just flowed.

Indeed, you are in the midst of the most romantic season of your life! Yes, marriage is awesome—but married life is different than the life you're experiencing right now. Don't get ahead of yourself and miss out on this special season of pre-engagement and engagement.

Call it love. Say, "I will." Start praying together, planning together, and dreaming together about a wonderful future. Enjoy these special days. They pass so quickly! Before you know it, you'll be saying, "I do" to your man worth keeping. And a whole new, marvelous chapter of life will begin.

TOMORROW IS ANOTHER *Day*

After spending two hours in heavy freeway traffic, I slumped into my parents' home, devastated once more. Another holiday, another broken heart. My grandparents had already arrived and could hardly ignore my puffy, tear-stained face. Grandpa George walked over to me and put his arm around my shoulder.

"Boy, Victorya, you sure do love deeply," he said.

For one brief moment, my pain disappeared, and hope filled my heart. God knew exactly what I needed to hear. Through Grandpa's simple words of love, I felt validated. Grandpa reinforced my shaken belief that I was indeed capable of love, even if it wasn't reciprocated. To find love, you must risk failure. I had done that. I had lost this time, but I knew I would risk again. In the words of Scarlett O'Hara, "After all . . . tomorrow is another day."

Romans 8:24–25 puts it this way: "Hope that is seen is no hope at all. Who hopes for what he already has? But if we hope for what we do not yet have, we wait for it patiently."

The ten secrets I've shared in this book are not easy to put into practice. I know. I've lived them. But oh, how worthwhile it has been to persevere and hold out for God's best!

If you have followed through and adapted these ten secrets into your life, you now love yourself enough to have identified what you want in a man. You've turned your life inside out, and you're having more fun than ever before. You've dared to take an honest look in the mirror, and you've emerged a swan. Because you've let the world know you're free, you're amazed at how much larger your dating pool has become.

Your life has been transformed by your choice to seek divine intervention in every area, including your husband search. Jesus is more real to you than ever before. You know he has your best interests at heart, and he is actively guiding your every step.

You've learned how easy it is to be a great date. Never again will you freak out or freak *him* out, because you no longer feel desperate, and you've developed other outlets for expressing your insecurities. You've set clear limits on passion. You've determined to face reality if your guy isn't "the one." Ultimately, when you and your man have had sufficient time to discover how you feel about one another, you know you will call it love or call it quits and stick with your decision.

Yes, you have become an attractive, self-assured, unique woman of God who knows her purpose in life and what kind of man will compliment that mission. Now you walk away early from dangerous men (even when it hurts) and risk your heart only with those who show potential. You have become a prize worth winning!

You've also become a woman of renewed hope. Despite past discouragements and failures, you believe again that if God's plan for you includes marriage, you absolutely *will* find your man worth keeping.

In fact, he may be near at this very moment. Or maybe even . . . already here.

E X T R A
S E C R E T S
FOR SINGLE
Moms

I couldn't end this book without offering a few more secrets for a special group of single women: women with children. If you're a single mom consumed with raising children, earning a living, and keeping a home—and still grasping onto the hope of finding love and a man worth keeping—here are some tips just for you.

SECRET 11
definitely KNOW WHAT YOU'RE LOOKING FOR

Even more than the average single gal, you need to know what you want in a prospective husband before you begin to date. I don't have to remind you how difficult it is to schedule a guilt-free evening away from the children. Yet in order to find a man worth keeping, you'll have to make time for a dating life. By knowing very clearly what you're looking for, you can make wiser choices about who gets to spend those precious moments with you.

Make sure you expanded your husband wish list to include an-swers to such questions as: How do you see a new man fitting into your current family? Do you want a man who already has children of his own? How many more children do you want to have, if any? Who will be the disciplinarian? Do you want a man who can be the sole breadwinner so you can stay home with the kids?

SECRET 12
DON'T HIDE THE FACT THAT YOU HAVE KIDS

Brett had been dating Michelle for a month when he was invited over to her house for dinner. As Brett was relaxing in her living room, he noticed a few photos of an adorable young boy and asked, "Is that your nephew?"

"No, that's my son," she responded.

Brett was so surprised that Michelle had, until that moment, de-liberately concealed something so significant that he abruptly ex-cused himself and left. He never called her again. Perhaps he could have been more gracious; but Michelle did herself, her son, and Brett a disservice with her "lie by omission."

Never keep the fact that you have children a secret. Yes, you're likely to narrow your field of potential suitors. But remem-ber, you are only looking for *one* man—one who wants you *and* your children.

SECRET 13
DON'T GIVE OUT YOUR HOME PHONE NUMBER

Give your dates a phone number other than your home line on which to call you. You don't want your children hearing romantic phone messages meant for Mom! Have your dates call you at work, on your cell phone, or on a separate voice-mail line. This isn't about hiding things from your children; it's about protecting their hopes and dreams for their family for as long as you can. You don't want to confuse or unsettle them unnecessarily or prematurely.

SECRET 14
DON'T RUSH TO INTRODUCE YOUR CHILDREN

While you need to be upfront with your date about the fact that you have children, wait until there is the genuine possibility of a future with this man before you introduce him to your kids. If you think a breakup is hard on grownups—people who've already had plenty of experience with disappointment—imagine how difficult it is on trusting children who tend to bond quickly and blame themselves when things go wrong. It's your job to protect their fragile hearts!

Besides, kids are rarely indifferent. They either want you to stay single, or they want you to get married right away; thus, every date is either a threat or a promise to them. Parenting has enough daily drama! Save yourself the added anxiety by waiting until the time is right to make introductions.

SECRET 15
HAVE THE FIRST MEETING WITH
THE KIDS ON NEUTRAL GROUND

When you are ready to introduce your man, think *comfortable* and *casual*. Don't make the first get-together a major event by telling your kids they are meeting someone very important to you. Keep their expectations low. After all, until they get to know your boyfriend and he gets to know them, you can't *really* be sure he's your man worth keeping.

Consider bringing him to a group event with other children and adults around so he can blend in. Try a kids-oriented restaurant, group picnic, amusement park, sporting event, or church activity. Choose something you know your kids will enjoy. If they're having fun and a new person just happens to be tagging along, it takes the pressure off everyone involved.

SECRET 16
CONSIDER DOING A BACKGROUND CHECK

Before you leave your boyfriend alone with your kids, have a background check done on him. Yes, I'm serious! God entrusted you with those babies. You need to protect them at all costs.

I mean, think how commonplace it has become for childcare facilities, schools, and even churches to perform background checks on employees and volunteers who will be working with kids. It's a shame it's necessary, but that's the world we live in today. Don't you think it would be wise to be at least as careful in your own home? Even if your boyfriend uses incredibly spiritual language and seems like the "perfect Christian," check him out anyway. Not every abuser or pedophile will be discovered through a background check, but it makes sense to do at least that much.

Background checks can easily be obtained through various Web sites or by going to your local courthouse and checking public records. Go back to secret 4 for the names of several good Internet sources. Your date should not be offended; most of us have had our backgrounds checked at one point or another, whether for a job or some other reason—perhaps without even knowing it. If your guy gets upset, simply explain that it's not an issue of a woman not trusting the man she is dating; it's an issue of a mother protecting her children. Your children have to come first. If you don't protect them, who will? A man worth keeping will understand.

SECRET 17
SEE HOW HE HANDLES "KIDDIE CHAOS"

Kids will be kids. No matter how great a disciplinarian you are or how angelic your precious children are most of the time, there will be times of "kiddie chaos." Before you commit forever to your man, you need to see how he handles unpleasant moments with your kids. It's one thing for a man to think he will enjoy having little ones around; it's another thing for him to actually experience the, shall we say, *diversity* of your precious children's behavior from day to day.

SECRET 18
WATCH HOW HIS FAMILY TREATS YOUR KIDS

Becky and Tom were planning to get married in February. Two months before the wedding, however, Becky and her five-year-old daughter, Olivia, joined Tom at a Christmas party with his extended family. That evening Tom's parents lavished each of their six biological grandchildren with four or five gifts each, but they gave nothing to Olivia. Becky was horrified. Tom was indifferent and later irritated that Becky would think anything inappropriate had occurred. Warning sirens went off loudly, and Becky made the wise, yet painful, decision to call off the wedding.

I'm happy to report that one year later, Becky met and eventually married a fabulous Christian man who loves Olivia every bit as much as if he had fathered her himself. Olivia is gushed over by his parents as well. Recently a baby brother was added to the family, and all four are doing great!

The moral of this story? Make sure you watch how your boyfriend's parents and extended family members treat your kids. Do they welcome them as part of the family, or do they treat them as outsiders? Remember, you don't just marry the man; you gain his entire extended family and all their baggage. Of course, you can't blame *him* for their inappropriate behavior. But if his family members behave unacceptably and he sees nothing wrong, run!

SECRET 19
DON'T LET HIM SPEND THE NIGHT OR DRINK ALCOHOL AROUND THE CHILDREN

I don't care how old or young your children are or how far away your date lives. It is never appropriate to have a man spend the night in your home, even if you have a guest room. It sets a bad example—one that may very well come back to haunt you later. If your guy is from out of town, have him stay in a hotel or with another friend. No exceptions!

And whatever stance you take on adult drinking, it is never a good idea to indulge around your children. If your date cannot abstain from drinking wine, beer, or hard liquor when your kids are around, then perhaps alcohol is too important to him.

SECRET 20
DON'T IGNORE RED FLAGS!

More than other single women, you cannot afford to allow loneliness or desperation to keep you from noticing "red flags" in your relationship. Your man is not just a potential husband; he's a potential father to your kids. Deliberately sharpen the skills we discussed in secret 9 so you can be prepared to face reality. You and your children have had enough heartache in your lives already. If your new man seems too good to be true, then maybe he is. If you get a funny feeling in the pit of your stomach when he says or does something, pay attention to those feelings. Tell a friend. Get feedback. And stay alert!

As a single mother, you have a unique road to travel. But that doesn't mean you have to keep traveling it alone. God may have other plans! If you follow these last ten secrets along with the first ten, you will not only guard your heart and protect your precious children; you'll be on the right track to finding a man worth keeping for you—and a dad worth keeping for your kids.

NOTES

INTRODUCTION: HOW THE SECRETS CAME TO BE

1. See Proverbs 16:9.

SECRET 2: TURN YOUR LIFE INSIDE OUT

1. Rick Warren, *The Purpose-Driven Life* (Grand Rapids: Zondervan, 2002), 30.

2. See Matthew 10:30 and Luke 12:7.

3. Bruce Wilkinson, *The Dream Giver* (Sisters, Ore.: Multnomah, 2003), 69.

4. Howard Dayton, *Your Money Counts: The Biblical Guide to Earning, Spending, Saving, Investing, and Getting Out of Debt* (Gainsville, Ga.: Crown Financial Ministries, 1996), 8.

SECRET 3: TAKE AN HONEST LOOK IN THE MIRROR

1. Dr. Marianne LaFrance, "University Study Concludes Hairstyles Make or Break Your First Impression," *Physique Stylezone Style News, February 21, 2001,* found at http://www.physique.com/usa/sn/sn_yale-study2.asp.

2. National Institute of Mental Health, "The Numbers Count" (2001), http://www.nimh.nih.gov/publicat/numbers.cfm.

3. La France, "University Study."

4. Ibid.

5. Carla Rice, "The Body Image Continuum: Exploring the Range of Body Image Problems," *Best Start,* 1995, found at http://www.beststart.org/resources/bdy_img/BIreport/Bodyimage4.html.

6. "Procedural Statistics Press Kit: More Than 8.7 Million Cosmetic Plastic Surgery Procedures in 2003," American Society of Plastic Surgeons, March 8, 2004, found at http://www.plasticsurgery.org/news_room/Procedural-Statistics-Press-Kit-Index.cfm. Also, "Quick Facts: Highlights of the ASAPS 2003 Statistics on Cosmetic Surgery," American Society for Aesthetic Plastic Surgery, 2003, found at http://www.surgery.org/press/procedurefacts-asqf.php.

SECRET 4: LET THE WORLD KNOW You're Free

1. Adapted from "Online Dating Tips" by Jim Clayton, founder of Christian Dating Service.com. His tips can be found at http://www.christiandatingservice.com/christian_dating.html.

2. Marco R. della Cava, "Truth in Advertising Hits Internet Dating," *USA Today,* April 20, 2004, D1.

3. Ibid.

4. Pat Allen and Sandra Harmon, *Getting To I Do* (New York: Avon, 1994), 98.

5. Information about Yogi Berra and a listing of some of his famous quotes can be found at http://www.yogi-berra.com/about.html and http://www.yogiberra.com/yogi-isms.html.

SECRET 5: SEEK DIVINE INTERVENTION

1. See 2 Corinthians 11:2 and Revelation 19:7.

2. Adapted from Jim and Karen Covell and Victorya Michaels Rogers, *How to Talk About Jesus without Freaking Out* (Sisters, Ore.: Multnomah, 2000), 128–29.

3. See Psalm 56:8 (NLT) and John 10:10.

4. See Philippians 4:6–7, Hebrews 13:5, and Jeremiah 29:11.

5. Just read the Psalms. King David was open and honest with God about all his emotions, including anger, yet God called him "a man after my own heart" (Acts 13:22).

6. See Matthew 7:7–11.

SECRET 6: BE A GREAT DATE

1. Ellen Fein and Sherrie Schneider, *The Rules: Time-Tested Secrets for Capturing the Heart of Mr. Right* (New York: Warner, 1995), 40, 45, 51.

2. Dale Carnegie, *How to Win Friends and Influence People* (New York: Simon & Schuster, 1936), 59.

3. Barbara Walters, *How to Talk with Practically Anybody about Practically Anything* (Garden City, N.Y.: Dell, 1970), 181–82.

4. Carnegie, *How to Win Friends and Influence People*, 94.

5. Walters, *How to Talk with Practically Anybody*, 165.

6. Ibid., 164.

7. Thomas W. McKnight and Robert Phillips, *Love Tactics: How to Win the One You Want* (Garden Park City, N.Y.: Avery, 1988), 21–22.

8. Ibid., 62.

9. Fein and Schneider, *The Rules*, 36–39.

SECRET 7: DON'T FREAK HIM OUT

1. Tim Timmons and Charlie Hedges, *Call It Love or Call It Quits: The Single's Guide to Meaningful Relationships* (Dallas: Word, 1988), Contents.

SECRET 8: KNOW YOUR LIMITS

1. John Gray, *Mars and Venus on a Date* (New York: HarperCollins, 1997), 155.

2. Ibid., 156–57.

3. McKnight and Phillips, *Love Tactics*, 108.

SECRET 9: FACE REALITY

1. Beth Moore, *A Woman's Heart: God's Dwelling Place* (Nashville: LifeWay, 1995), 140.

SECRET 10: CALL IT LOVE OR CALL IT QUITS

1. See Hebrews 13:5.

2. Karen S. Peterson, "Forgiveness Could Be Balm for the Body, Too," *USA Today*, October 22, 2003.

3. See Luke 1:37.